mountain, get out
of my way

mountain, get out of my way

LIFE LESSONS AND LEARNED TRUTHS

MONTEL WILLIAMS

with daniel paisner

WARNER BOOKS

A Time Warner Company

Warner Books, Inc., 1271 Avenue of the Americas, New York, NY 10020

W A Time Warner Company

Printed in the United States of America
First Printing: March 1996
10 9 8 7 6 5 4 3 2

Library of Congress Cataloging-in-Publication Data

Williams, Montel.
    Mountain, get out of my way: life lessons and learned truths / Montel Williams,
with Daniel Paisner.
    p. cm.
    ISBN 0-446-51907-3
    1. Conduct of life. 2. Ethics—United States. 3. Self-efficacy.
4. Williams, Montel. I. Paisner, Daniel. II. Title.
BJ1581.2.W55 1996   95-31318
248.8'6—dc20   CIP

Book design by L & G McRee

To the women in my life:

my manager, Melanie McLaughlin;
my attorney, Nina Shaw;
my mother-in-law, Dori Kotzan;
my mother, Marjorie Williams;
my daughters—Ashley, Maressa and Wynter-Grace;
and my wife, Gracie

CONTENTS

*If ye have faith as a grain of mustard
seed, ye shall say unto this mountain,
Remove hence to yonder place; and it shall
remove; and nothing shall be impossible unto you.*
THE HOLY BIBLE
Matthew 17:20

1

Mountain, Get out of My Way

Before you read any further, know this: chances are, you will not agree with everything I have to say in these pages. In fact, I'm sure of it. At some point, somewhere in here, you're going to have a problem with something I write. Count on it.

This, I believe, is a good thing. If it goes the way I think it will go, it will mean I'm getting through to every last one of you, at least on some level. If it goes some other way, if these pages can't trigger some powerful emotional response, then it will mean I haven't accomplished what I set out to do.

And what is that? Well, for this book at least, I'm out to shake you up, to get you to reflect on some of your fundamental beliefs—on race, religion, work, family, education, urban violence, drug abuse, child abuse, spousal abuse and every other kind of abuse there is in this world. I take this upon myself because it needs doing, and because it was what I was put here to do. I do this because after addressing more than three million students, parents and young adults across the country over the past seven years, I have become astonished at the lack of direction and motivation in our society. I do this because if nobody baits you into taking a stand, you might never stand up for what you believe.

My own beliefs are fairly straightforward, and not uncommon. If you believe in something else, that's fine. If you reject any of my beliefs, that's fine too, but here they are: I believe in God. I believe in love and family. I believe in education. I believe in hard work and dedication. I believe in restraint, responsibility and respect. I believe in love and romance. And I believe in setting goals and reaching them. There is nothing you can't do if you set your mind to it.

The title of this book underlines my conviction and has been a constant theme of my life: "Mountain, get out of my way." It's a line I first heard in Marine Corps boot camp, back in 1974. I had a drill instructor who used to say it all the time. He got it from an old gospel song, but it comes originally from the New Testament, in a passage that concludes, "nothing shall be impossible unto you" (Matthew 17:20). By the time I left boot camp it was a part of me. I've woven the phrase through every speech I've ever given, and I will invoke it here at every chance. There is no more important message. If you have faith, you can move mountains. If you have faith in something bigger than yourself—in God, community, family, whatever—then anything is possible. Faith alone will give you the strength to clear any obstacle in your way.

Now, while I'm on the subject of faith, here's my first chance to sound off: I firmly believe that the movement to take God out of our public schools has had a more disastrous impact on contemporary American society than any other legislative action of the past thirty years. I don't care what kind of God you pray to, or even if you pray at all, but the moment we started telling our children it was no longer okay to express their beliefs, whatever their beliefs, that there was no room in their school days for even silent, disorganized prayer, was the very moment we opened the door to a lot of the problems we're facing today.

Consider the message we've given our children. Religion is insignificant; you can't pray here; your beliefs, whatever they are, don't belong in this public place. The message took, and after so many years it's become almost unfashionable to be a religious person. And it's gone deeper than that. This glaring lack of faith among our young people has become one of the root causes of most of our societal ills, and this is one of our great shames. When we took God out of our schools, we also took away the belief in something bigger than ourselves. We told our children there were no such things as restraint, responsibility and respect. Our actions spoke louder than any words to the contrary.

Too many high school kids today don't see any ramifications to the choices they make. To some, the space between right and wrong is too narrow to find; most don't bother to look; some don't recognize it when they step in it. Our children are sleepwalking through adolescence, without a clue. Their time on this planet has no weight, no valence, no meaning. They have no concept of a higher being or a common good, and I have to think this somehow flows from the mixed signals we've been sending. To a lot of these kids, there's no reason not to go out and take a life, or bust up a store, or pump one killing substance or another through their veins, because for them it's already over. There's nothing left for them to do but check out and phone it in.

I'll never forget when I first made this connection. It troubled me then and it troubles me still. I was making a presentation at a high school in Jackson, Mississippi, back when they were just starting to have some serious gang problems there. For a time, before I resigned my commission from the U.S. Navy in order to devote my full energies to public speaking, I dressed in uniform for these appearances, and on this occasion my full Navy garb was not nearly enough to impress this one kid in the audience.

Nothing I did made an impression. He rode me all through my talk, and he lingered long after I was through. After my presentation, I stayed behind to visit with a couple hundred students who wanted to hear more, and this kid still wouldn't go away.

Finally, we had it out. "You have something to say, then say it," I yelled at him.

"Ooooh," he mocked, pretending to be afraid. "Listen to Mr. Baldy."

"That's right," I said. "Listen to Mr. Baldy, because what I've got to say can keep your ass out of jail."

"Why should I listen to you?" he shot back. Then he hit me again before I could answer: "How much money you got in your pocket?"

"What?" I snapped. It was unusual for a high school kid to challenge me, a naval officer, in just this way, and I wasn't sure I'd heard right.

"You heard me," he repeated. "How much money you got in your pocket?"

Yes, I heard him, but I wasn't sure how to answer. I wanted to buy myself some time, to think how to play this exchange. The principal and one or two of the teachers went to silence the kid, but I waved them away. If I couldn't make my point with him, I had no business being up on that stage. I thought the best tack was to answer him, see where he was going, find some way to turn him around.

I used to give away money during my presentations—to prove the point that education and knowledge do pay off in real terms—and I had about forty dollars on me. I reached into my pocket to show the few bills I had left. Then the kid reached into his pocket and pulled out the fattest wad of money I'd ever seen. He had the money rolled up neat and tight, and then he fanned it out for all to see. There was a thousand-dollar bill on the outside, hugging hundreds and twenties on the inside. There must have been eight thousand, easy.

He walked up to the auditorium stage and put the roll on a table, for emphasis. "I got this," he said. Then he pointed to me. "You got that." Then he laughed.

"You tell me to go to school because it'll make me money down the road, but I got more money right here than you'll probably make in the next five months."

He was right about that, but he was all wrong about everything else. Trouble was, he now had the couple hundred remaining students with him, and I knew if I couldn't rein him in, I'd lose the crowd, and whatever ground I'd gained during my presentation. This kid might be a lost cause, but I wanted the others. They stayed behind because they needed help, not because they wanted to see me battle wits with a fool.

He kept at it. "How many bitches you got?" he asked.

Again, I wasn't sure I'd heard right: "What do you mean, how many bitches I got?" Now it was clear where he was going, but I couldn't seem to redirect him. I worried the kid was better at his game than I was at mine.

"I mean how many bitches you got?"

I was separated from my first wife, in the process of getting a divorce, but there was one person I was seeing. "I have a girlfriend," I said.

"Me," he said, "I got more ass than I can pop. I get it every day." By this point, the other kids were cheering wildly each time this kid put me down.

"How many cars you got?"

At the time, I was driving a Toyota MR2, which I thought was kind of a nice car, and I told him.

"Me," the kid said, "I got a BMW sittin' out there, and tomorrow, me and my homeys are going down to buy a Mercedes." The kid was sixteen years old, a real gang-banger, and he was all over me. Like a fool, I let him run his mouth. "So you tell me, Mr. Baldy," he continued, "you tell me why I should listen to you. I got bitches. I got money. I got cars. If I die tomorrow, I've had it all. What difference does it make?"

There. I finally had my opening. The kid just unlocked the door and held it wide: *if I die tomorrow.* "Hold on," I said. "What if you don't die tomorrow? What happens then? What if The Man locks your ass up and throws you in jail?" I started ripping into this kid like the drill instructor he needed, trying to make up the ground I'd lost. "He's gonna put a two-dollar pair of underwear on your behind, and a dollar T-shirt on your back, and some big dude's gonna pull your shorts down as soon as the lights go out. What difference does it make? You tell me what difference it makes."

I had the crowd back after this, but there was no getting through to this kid. "Still don't make no difference," he said. "I'm not goin' to jail. They're gonna take me out. I'm goin' down."

I've heard the same story a thousand times since, and underneath the tragedy I keep coming back to God and school. The kids I talk to don't believe in God because we've told them not to believe in God, and now they've got nothing to hold on to. Do I think the freedom—better, the encouragement—to believe in God would have made a difference in their lives? Maybe, maybe not. But even a small child who goes to church or synagogue, not knowing why he's there, knows enough to understand *something.* He knows that the people around him have placed their hearts and souls in a place where virtue is rewarded, where you must atone for your sins, where good triumphs over evil. He knows that he matters.

This, I believe, marks the beginning of the deterioration of the American family, and without family this country has just spun out of control. It's as good an explanation as any for why we are the way we are, and I think it all falls from there.

It goes back to the point I made earlier. Once we legislated religion out of everything, we had to replace it with something else, so money and success became the gospel. States wiped the blue laws off their books. The lottery ticket became a true pass to everlasting peace. Before we knew it, we were a society of people looking to trade our work ethic for an easy payday. All of a sudden, it wasn't good enough to be a hardworking person, making a living, supporting a family. Now we all have to be millionaires, and we have to be millionaires right away. Everyone's looking for shortcuts, but there are no shortcuts, not a single one.

When I go down this path in one of my talks, someone from the audience will invariably challenge me. "Look at you," they'll say. "You've got a talk show. You've got money. Who are you to talk?"

I'll tell you who I am to talk. I'm the youngest of four children, born when and where it wasn't easy for a black man to earn an honest living. I'm the product of a loving home, splintered by tension and frustration. My father worked three or four jobs throughout my growing up. My mother worked two. They barely had time for themselves, let alone for us kids. My sisters and brother and I all worked when we were old enough. We went to church every Sunday. We ate dinner together most evenings. There were no shortcuts.

That's what this book is about. It's not about me so much as it is about where I have been and where we are all going. It's about the mountains I have moved out of my way and the ones that may be standing in yours. I don't have all the answers, but I know what questions to ask and I know what rings true. I can look back on the choices I've made—some good, some bad—and learn from them.

I can hold a mirror to the world that passes before me and see what I see.

2

Baltimore

I was born in 1956, the last of four children. We lived in a row house on Southland Avenue in Cherry Hill, Baltimore, at the low end of a low-income neighborhood. It was a place that shaped me in more ways than I can know.

My father had been a bus driver, but by the time I arrived he was a full-time fireman and a part-time carpenter and musician. He helped to break the color line in the Baltimore Fire Department, doing shift work as a pump operator for next to nothing. There was a separate pay scale for blacks, but my father accepted it because at least it was a kind of progress. Before the 1950s, most black neighborhoods had their own fire departments, and most of them didn't have any equipment. They just trained people to take buckets from a lake and throw water on a house. Now, at least, my father could help ensure his family and friends were properly protected and build a career for himself at the same time, even if he had to start on the lowest rung. He may have been underpaid, relative to his colleagues, and some of the other inequities were tough for him to take, but it was respectable, honest work.

The long, uncertain shifts must have also been difficult, but they were a part of the job, for blacks and whites. And the work didn't end with each shift. On nights he was off duty, my father played bass and sang in a jazz and Top 40 band on the club circuit, from Washington, D.C., to Atlantic City. When his days were free, he hauled cement, swung a hammer and laid bricks, whatever kind of construction work he could find, wherever he could find it. He probably did every job that you could as a builder, and he was never certified for a single one of them, but he could drive around town and admire his projects with the pride of a craftsman.

My mother was a nurse's aide. She was also a laborer in some of the nearby factories and eventually worked as a technician at Bendix, and later at Westinghouse, where she remained for some time. She was always working at least one job, sometimes two. She was out of the house by the time we all left for school, but she was usually home when I got back at the end of the day.

Our building was right around the corner from the city incinerator, and that was our playground. We'd

spend hours sneaking around the incinerator and hiding inside it. One of our favorite games was to shoot
rats with BB guns and slingshots. Actually, the bigger
kids would do all the shooting. They would make us
little kids run through the dump to chase the rats out,
and whenever we got one, we'd take it by the tail and
throw it up into a tree.

What I remember best about Cherry Hill during this
period, 1958 to 1962, was the poverty of the place,
and my "playground" memories only reinforce this for
me. It was a real ghetto. The only time I saw a white
face was through the back window of our car, when we
had to go outside our neighborhood to buy something.
I'd never get out of the car, but I'd look out and know
there was another world out there, another way to live.
I'd also know, from the return gazes I'd receive through
the glass, that we were treading in a place where we
didn't quite belong.

When I was six years old, we moved to a neighborhood called Morris Hill, in Glen Burnie, a suburb just
south of the city. Now we were at the high end of a
lower- to middle-class black community. We were
moving up in the world. My father had collected
enough surplus building supplies from his odd jobs to
rough-in a small house for us. He'd set aside some
money too, in working three jobs, and he was able to
get a mortgage and a builder friend to help him out. He
finished off the living room, kitchen and a couple of
bedrooms within a few months, and he put all of us to
work over the next ten years or so, finishing off the rest
of the place. We were like a live-in crew. I learned how
to mix cement, how to find something level, how to

hold a board in place. We even helped put in a swimming pool, and that pool was a big deal to my father, a symbol. He was actually afraid of the water and never swam in it, but that wasn't the point. He wanted a house in the suburbs, with some land and a pool in the ground, and he busted his ass to get it.

I clearly inherited my father's drive and work ethic, but he never sat me down and laid these out for me in plain terms. I learned by his example. He was always working. He saw what he wanted and knew the only way to get it was to work for it. When he wanted more, he found time to go to night school, for a bachelor's degree. Here again, he set the tone. Education was important to him, but he never had to spell it out for us. He just went to school and studied hard. That's what you did in our house.

You also went to church. Every Sunday, no matter what you were out doing the night before. I was even an altar boy for a while. Most of the time I went willingly, although as I got older I started to resent having to go. These days, I no longer think of myself as a Roman Catholic, although that's how I was raised, but I believe in God and I believe in the Bible. I'll never lose my faith. I pray on my own, in my own way. I still go to church from time to time, and I will always consider myself a spiritual person, and I'm sure it goes back to all those Sunday mornings as a kid.

We weren't a God-fearing family so much as a God-respecting one. I grew up knowing the difference between right and wrong. I understood the concept of sin, even if I didn't always adhere to it.

At home, my parents went to a lot of trouble not to

let us know how poor we truly were. Even after we moved to Glen Burnie, money was tight. There was always enough for music lessons at school or to send us for a couple weeks to a summer day camp run at the Fort Meade Army Base, but my parents cut some corners when they had to. A half dozen eggs went a long way in our house. I can remember times when, for a week and a half, dinner would be milk and pancakes. Or two hot dogs split among four kids. Then there'd be some food in the house and everything would be okay for a while, but a couple weeks later we'd be back to cereal or French toast. That was the way it was pretty much until I entered junior high school, until my father's night schooling began to pay off and he started getting promoted a little bit at the fire department.

We kids didn't know any better, or different, and it was in many respects a comfortable, nurturing environment. We had it better than most. My mother saw to it that we were always properly fed and nicely clothed. She worked throughout my childhood, but she was always around to dispense hugs and Band-Aids and whatever else it was we desperately needed. It was my mother who was dragged from work and down to school whenever one of us was getting jammed by the principal. Usually, this was a result of something my brother or I had done (or something we hadn't done and were just suspected of doing), and we could not have hired a better advocate for all the money in the world. She stood up to the principal like no other mother I knew, and ran interference for her children whenever she thought we weren't getting a fair shake.

With my father around, though, my mother was

almost a different person. She'd never stand up to him, not even for her children, which sometimes made our house a very scary place. By today's standards, some people might call my father an abusive parent, although I never saw him that way. I still don't. Maybe my brother and sisters saw him differently. I can't speak for them, but I think I saw him for what he truly was: a disciplinarian, from the old school. It's easy to forget, but there was a different ethic in place back then. My father was authoritative and tough. That's the way he was raised. Things were done his way or not at all. He commanded respect. And he whupped his kids when we got out of line. He ruled his house with an iron hand, and we were all powerless against it, my mother most of all.

One of the side benefits to being the youngest of four children is that you have a chance to take everything in before you have a chance to make a mistake. I've talked to thousands of families, from some of the most abusive households imaginable, and in almost every case the youngest child has had the easiest time of it. That was the way it was for me, although "easy" is probably not the right word. It was more simple than easy, and it was simple because I had the time to figure things out. I saw my older sister bring home a bad report card and get whupped. I saw my brother forget to do his chores and get whupped. I heard my other sister raise her voice in anger and get whupped. I learned the drill. Don't get bad grades. Don't forget to vacuum. Don't talk back. These were the bottom lines, and I tried to hold to them.

Of course, I wasn't always successful. I took my

share of whuppings. I made the same kinds of mistakes that a lot of kids make today. I hooked school, as often as not. I smoked a little dope. I drank some beer and raised some hell. I did a lot of stupid things, especially in high school. One of our favorite stupid things to do was grab a six-pack of beer and sit in the train tunnels, waiting for a train to come down the tracks; then we'd race the train to the open end, and if we couldn't make it, we'd lie flat against the wall as it went by. Or we'd get drunk and go out driving on a dark road with no headlights. We were a bunch of idiots, with some of the stuff we did, and it's amazing to me that nobody was ever seriously hurt. We could have been, though, and what's frightening is that these kinds of stunts are nothing next to some of the lunatic things some kids are up to today.

I may have been beat for some of the reckless things we did, but my parents and teachers never caught up with most of my less dangerous delinquent behavior. I was pretty inventive when it came to not being where I was supposed to be. In high school, I was active in student government and all kinds of school activities, so I was always able to come up with a believable excuse for missing class. I was a good student, and the teachers knew I was on the student council, or president of my class, or whatever, so they didn't think twice.

With my parents, I had to be even more resourceful. My strategy was to steer clear as much as possible, but I always had to account for my time. By high school, when I was old enough to make real trouble, I was playing in a band and had my parents thinking our

21

gigs were ending up at two or three o'clock in the morning, when really we broke at midnight, leaving me a couple hours to hang out without fear of reprisal. In the afternoons, I was busy with so many sanctioned activities, like student government, band practice, and after-school jobs, that there was always a reason not to come home. I'd be flipping burgers at some fast-food joint, washing cars on a car lot, working odd jobs in the neighborhood, as much for an excuse to stay out of the house as to earn some extra money. My parents never knew where I was supposed to be.

The trick to coming home was not to be there when my father got back from a shift. That was always a tense time. He used to park his car across the street, in the shade, and sit there for an hour or so, waiting for one rage or another to pass. Something always happened at work to set him off, and he knew enough to decompress a little bit before coming inside. I'd watch him from my window and hope he would stay across the street until he cooled out. It didn't always work. Four or five times a week, there'd be no problem, but on that sixth or seventh day he'd come into the house and take whatever it was out on one of us. If any of us screwed up, it was over, so I tried to stay in line or out of sight. This didn't always work either, but I got beat a whole lot less than any of my siblings, and a whole lot less than I deserved.

When I was little enough to fit, I'd hide out in the cabinet of this old television console unit to escape my father's attention. The picture tube was shot, and my father was always meaning to repair it, but the set remained in our living room for as long as I can remember, waiting for my father to get to it. I'd climb in and sit myself in the box behind the screen and peer out into the room at the rest of my family. This strikes me now as an odd metaphor for what I have gone on to do for a living—examining dysfunctional families on a television talk show—but at the time, the inside of our television set was a great place to disappear. I could see everybody else and nobody could see me.

School was another convenient hiding place—once I got used to it and it got used to me. Unfortunately, this took a while. Glen Burnie was mostly a white community in Anne Arundel County, but we lived in a small black subdivision called Morris Hill. From there, we were bused to a predominantly white school a couple miles away. In fact, busing started the year we moved in, and it wasn't an easy transition for any of us. To my parents, this meant opportunity, a chance at a better education. To us kids, it was a cold new reality. From the beginning, it was made absolutely clear to us that we were being sent where we weren't wanted.

Even at six years old, in first grade, I got this sense from the other kids, from the parents, and from the teachers. There were no blacks in my school, other than the janitors and cafeteria workers, and that had just been fine with everybody there. The very first day of school, one of the teachers called me a nigger while I was out on the playground, and I would hear it again almost every day after that. I knew what the word meant, but I'd never heard it spoken by a white person in such a hateful way, and I learned then that words could have entirely different meanings depending on who spoke them. I learned what it was like to have to go where you weren't wanted.

It was a very confusing time. Just a few of my friends from my neighborhood were bused to the same school, so I pretty much stayed to myself for the first couple years. I found that by working hard in class I could at least deflect some of the hostilities of my teachers. Some, but not all. There was one teacher who had a real problem with me, and she left her mark. When I was eight years old, I won a little community award for a story I'd written, and I was asked to write a story every couple weeks to be read on a local radio station.

It was a tremendous honor, to me, although it was obvious my third-grade teacher would have preferred one of her white students be singled out for the attention. She made this known in a number of not-so-subtle ways, the least subtle of which came around Christmastime, when I handed in a story about some gifts that I needed to get wrapped, and made an entirely innocent spelling mistake. Instead of "wrapped," I wrote "raped," and the woman was all over me for it. She circled the word in red and put a big "F" on the top of my paper.

I was devastated. I'd never gotten anything less than an "A" or "Great Job!" on the tops of my papers before, and even with the red circling, I still had no idea that I'd done anything wrong. So I went up to the teacher after class and asked what was wrong with my story. She looked back at me, cold, and said, "That's the reason why you people will never be nothin' in life. You only have one thing on your mind." That was all she said, and I never forgot it.

It was a few years before I figured out what she meant, but the sting of that moment stayed with me. I took the paper home and hid it under my mattress. I don't know why I didn't just throw it out. I guess I figured my father would see it in the garbage can or something. And I didn't dare ask my parents what my teacher might have meant. I knew I'd get beat if I brought home an F, even if it was a grade I didn't deserve or understand. (A couple months later, after realizing that my mother flipped my mattress every once in a while, I moved the story to my closet, and it stayed there until I was in junior high school.)

When we learned how to use a dictionary, I looked up the word "raped" and it finally hit me. This woman had it in her nasty little head that, at eight years old, the only things on my mind were sex and rape and violence. By "you people" she clearly meant "you black people," and I wasn't too young to recognize the enmity in her words.

It made me sick to my stomach, even then. It makes me sicker now. I still can't believe an educated woman in such a position could have been so ignorant and spiteful. At the time, I was so upset I actually closed the dictionary and asked to be sent to the nurse's office. The nurse was a kind woman, but she saw there was nothing wrong with me and sent me back to class. I couldn't tell her what was really bothering me.

Later, at lunch, one of the cafeteria workers noticed I was dragging my feet a little bit. This was a lady who tried to look out for me and the few other black kids in the school. "What's with you today, Montel?" she asked.

"One of my teachers said something to me about my color," I said. "It's got me pretty upset."

She put down what she was doing and walked over to me. "People are gonna say something about your color for the rest of your life" she said. "You just got to get beyond it."

And I did. This third-grade teacher stood as the first true mountain in my path, and if I hadn't bumped into her when I did, I might have taken a different road. I have no idea where it would have taken me. I might have been a successful person, but I don't think I would have been as driven, and I don't think my successes would have meant as much. I am not grateful to this teacher in any way, because I will never accept the mean-spirited way she treated me, but I do concede her role. That I was able to get beyond her had more to do with all the positive reinforcement I'd received in school up until that time than it did with the obstacle she presented. If I didn't have that base, I would probably have felt like an absolute failure. I might never have moved my first mountain. I would have become angry at everybody. I would have started to fulfill this woman's low expectations of me.

The fact that I even had to consider some of these issues points to one of the glaring problems in our society. This teacher was just ahead of her time, or behind the times, or however you want to look at it. Teachers today have the same bent, and I worry they'll never lose it. A black kid walks into an elementary school and right away his teachers are thinking, He's from a bad environment, He hasn't had the same breaks as the other children, We have to ride him extra hard if he's going to get ahead. I don't know whether it's a purely racist reaction, or if maybe there's some other trigger at work, but I see it all the time. We're too quick to label our children "At Risk" or "Special Needs" simply because of the color of their skin, or their economic background, or the fact that many are growing up in splintered families. I have a real problem with the concept, and it starts with the terminology. If you ask me, the only thing most of these kids are "at risk" of is succeeding.

The smartest minds in the country tell us that a child will live up or down to your expectations, and yet we still expect little from our black children. My story could have been a case in point, but I wouldn't let it. If I hadn't had those early accomplishments on which to build, if my parents hadn't instilled a sense of pride and entitlement, I probably would have been as bitter and unfocused as a lot of black kids today. But I knew enough to know that this third-grade teacher was the one with the problem, not me. I'd been stroked enough for my stories, or my drawing, or my music, to where my self-image didn't live or die on the hateful ignorance of one woman. Other kids aren't so lucky, but I was lucky.

The tension with my third-grade teacher didn't begin or end with this one failing grade. She was on me all year long about one thing or another. It's possible I was reading more into her behavior than was really there, but I don't think so. She was warm and affectionate with the other kids, but never with me. She returned their homework assignments gently, often with a kind word or two, but she would just toss my papers back on my desk without saying anything. She'd hug the other kids when they got hurt, but she would never touch me. She didn't like the way I wrote my *ns* even though my *ns* looked more like *ns* than most of the other kids', but my assignments were the only ones to come back with every *n* circled in red. This woman wasn't trying to toughen me up in any way, or build my character, or make me strong. She wasn't being helpful. She spent that entire school year looking down her nose at me, resentful that I was even in her class.

I'll never forget this teacher, and I'll never forgive her. She knows who she is. She may still be teaching, for all I know, and that's why we have some of the problems we have today. There are teachers like her in every mixed school in the country, at every level. Ignorance I can forgive, but hatred is another thing, and I will never abide such racist thinking in our public schools. It would be nice if we could erase it entirely, but if we at least eliminate that mind-set among our young people, it might just pass through our society and die of old age.

There was another racial incident that helped to shape me at a very early age—and set the stage for a complete reexamination of who I was and what I believed. I was a little older, about eleven, and this other kid started calling me names in the back of the class. He called me a nigger, and I called him honky trash. There really was no equivalent to "nigger," but "honky trash" was what I came up with.

Anyway, the teacher heard the whole argument, all the kids in the class were in on it, yet I was the one who was sent to the principal's office. My mother had to come to school to pick me up and listen to the principal tell her all about her racist son. He didn't mention anything about the other kid.

Well, my mother stood up for me in front of the principal, just like she always did, but she was furious when we got home. She hit me, for the first time I could remember, and it felt like I deserved it. She didn't explain herself; she just gave me the back of her hand.

And my father, when he got home, he just about tore me up. I kept saying, "Look, I didn't do anything, this kid started it," whatever, but it didn't matter. I never knew whether or not my parents respected me for standing up the way I did, because it didn't matter. What mattered was that I had embarrassed them, and that's why I got the beatings. The message that sunk in was that I was on my own in this matter. Whatever difficulty I had with the other kids at school, my parents didn't want to hear about it. I was to deal with my problems without them, and without getting in trouble.

As it turned out, the message was a bit more complicated, but it took a while to get to it. It took a while because my parents weren't the kind of people to sit us down and really talk through a situation. We never discussed the fact that we were the only black kids in an all-white school. They weren't interested in addressing the problems of racist America with their children. Or maybe they were, but it was plainly difficult for them.

I'd overhear my father tell my mother how it got to him that he had to sleep in a separate area from the whites at the fire house, but that was as far as it went. I can't remember a time when either one of my parents uttered a racial comment about whites when they thought one of us kids was listening, and it took this incident for me to discover why.

That afternoon, I learned that my grandmother on my mother's side was white, and the news pretty much floored me. It had never come up before that my mother was of mixed blood, and now that it had I was shocked. Not shocked as in ashamed or humiliated, but genuinely surprised. If my older siblings knew, they never let on. It was something I wished I had known sooner, something I wished we could have talked about. Suddenly, things started to make sense. It was okay for my father to curse and rant about the way some of the whites were treating him at work, but it was not okay for me to do the same over the way I was being treated at school. The difference was that I had my mother's blood running through my veins while my father did not, and that, I guess, made all the difference in the world.

So that was the first and last time my mother hit me. The last time my father hit me was a few years later, when I was fifteen, and to tell you the truth, I no longer remember what I did to deserve a whupping. Neither does he. But what I do remember is telling myself that this man would never raise his hand to me again. I loved my father, and I respected his values, but I was too old for him to slap me around when things didn't go his way. I had reached my limit. I was so outraged over this last beating that I picked myself up and ran away from home. This wasn't something you did in our house, but I did it anyway. I went to Ocean City, which at the time was probably the most racist city in Maryland. It was only about ninety miles from Baltimore, but it was like another planet to a fifteen-year-old black kid.

I don't know why I chose to go to Ocean City, but that's where I went. Somehow, I managed to talk my way into a job as an apprentice chef at a restaurant called the Ship's Cafe. I knew I had to work to eat, and I figured if I worked around food, I could probably eat pretty well—and save some of my money, besides. At night, I slept under the boardwalk by the restaurant. I stayed for about three weeks, and my parents were just flipping out back home. I spoke to some of my friends on the phone, and they told me how hot my folks were over my leaving, so I figured I'd stay a little longer and give them a chance to cool off.

When I finally came home, I knew I'd be in for a beating, but I was determined to stand up to my father. I walked in the door expecting this big confrontation.

"So, you think you're a big shot?" my father said. He was mad, but he wasn't moving to hit me.

"No, sir," I said.

"Did you think about what you put your mother through?" he asked.

"No, sir," I answered. I had, but not in the way he meant.

Then he asked me where I was for three weeks, and I told him. I handed over the money I'd saved while I was gone—about $450.

31

He said, "I don't want your money."

"No, sir," I insisted. "Take it."

I put the money on the table. My father got up and left the room. He didn't touch the money. It was spread out on the table until he left for work the next morning. We never said another word about it, but he didn't hit me that night, and he never hit me again.

3

Annapolis

For all my drive and ambition, I had no real direction in high school, and it would be some time before I knew where I was headed.

When I thought about it at all—and my problem was I rarely thought about it at all—I suppose I wanted to someday work in a technical field. I had visions of being everything from an engineer to an astronaut, but I had no clear path in mind.

I also had no fixed timetable. Going straight to a four-year university was almost out of the question, for a couple of reasons. For one, money was tight, and I knew I'd either have to go to a community college for a while or bank enough money over the next year or two so I could sit back and go to school without worrying about the bill. For another, I was getting kind of a bum steer from the high school guidance counselors who were purportedly there to help me figure my next move. I was a good student, I was class president and active in all kinds of extracurricular activities, but these people were selling me on trade schools and technical schools. It didn't matter that I had done all these things or that I was a good student. What mattered was that I was black and that I was bused in from Glen Burnie. That's all these people could see.

As a result, I never got the kind of advice my peers were getting, and by the time I woke up to the problem it was too late. I don't mean to lay this off on someone else, because in the end we are all accountable for our own missteps, but that's the way it happened. Application deadlines had come and gone. This was a mountain I should have anticipated, but now that it was upon me, it seemed I couldn't get past it, at least not right away. The only thing I could do was chart my own course. Going to college had always been a given, in my own head, and it remained a given. I just had to figure how to fit it in and how to pay for it.

My first thought was to let my music pay my way. I had been playing in a band all through high school. I'd never be a rock star, I knew, but I could certainly milk a good thing. We were making decent money. Some weekends, maybe every couple of months, I'd take home about $800, sometimes more. Back in the early 1970s that was a whole lot of money. It still is, for a high school kid. We had a gig almost every weekend, and some weeks we'd be booked Thursday through

Sunday nights. We'd play wherever we could, all around the Baltimore and Washington, D.C. areas, and as far away as Philadelphia and Atlantic City.

We were actually pretty good. We called ourselves Front Row. I sang and played bass and trumpet. We played mostly Top 40 and classic rock covers, but we also did some original material. We had a loyal local following. Everyone in the band was a few years older than me, and a couple of the guys were married, so we had to book our dates around my high school stuff. I felt a little childish, to be the only one still in school, the only one with a curfew, but there was no denying the benefits. Not too many high school kids could come up with a legitimate excuse to go out partying on school nights, and none were pulling down the kind of money I was. The money was actually great, but up until this time I'd blown most of it on clothes and parties. If I was going to start saving for school, I'd have to be a little more diligent and a little less indulgent, so I put myself on a budget, thinking it would take maybe two or three years before I'd have enough put away for college.

That was the plan, until it unraveled on me. It came undone pretty fast. In April of my senior year, just about the time my classmates were finding out what colleges had accepted them, a few of the guys in the band ran into some big trouble. They'd gotten into the bad habit of visiting certain convenience stores in the area, late at night, and ripping off a couple six-packs. They'd knock things off the shelves, scare the managers on duty, and basically act like menacing pains in the butt. It was petty stuff, and a lot of the kids I knew were doing the same thing all over town, but I stayed away just the same. I did my share of stupid things in high school, but my parents didn't raise me to be a vandal or to make trouble at someone else's expense.

The big trouble my friends made was this: one night, a few of the guys were busted taking some money from a store cash register, and the band immediately drifted apart. The rest of us thought we would somehow be implicated by association, even though we were probably home in bed at the time of the incident. Virtually overnight, we went from being a happening local band to having nothing at all to do with each other, while I went from having a loose plan for the future to having no plan at all. This was not a good thing. One moment, I had it all figured out; the next, I had no idea.

Around this time, I started to notice one of my brother's friends, a guy who had been a real screwup in high school. He'd apparently decided to straighten himself out by enlisting in the Marine Corps, and from what I could see, the experience changed him completely—and all for the good. He came back to school to talk about the G.I. Bill and the Vietnam War, and I caught myself really listening to what he had to say. It was what he said and how he said it. He held his head high and made himself heard. We spent some time afterward talking about the military and the chance for a government-sponsored education, and I was impressed by the way this guy had turned his life around. I began to think that maybe the Marine Corps could provide my ticket to a college education, and maybe give me some direction in the bargain.

I didn't talk to my parents all that much about it, because I didn't know that they had all that much to tell me. In my house, we didn't always talk things through. I knew my folks would be pleased I was pursuing an education, and I thought that was enough. I also knew they'd be proud to see me serve our country, and I thought that was gravy. It was a decision I had to make for myself.

I enlisted the following week and was assigned to boot camp at Parris Island, in South Carolina. Before I left, I spent my last free summer working in a local restaurant, putting away some money and getting my play out of my system. I also spent a lot of time worrying about boot camp and picking the brain of my brother's friend, trying to figure what I needed to know. I passed countless hours staring down a spot on the wall of my bedroom at home, standing at unflinching attention, trying to prepare myself for even the most demanding drill instructor. I wanted to be ready.

Boot camp was a demanding and exhilarating ordeal. For the most part, I relished my time there. It defined me and set me on a course for a disciplined life. It forced me to reevaluate who I was and what I stood for, taught me how to set goals and accomplish them and how to make the best of a difficult situation. Our days were plenty difficult. We couldn't talk to the other troops for the first nine weeks we were there. If you got away with a whispered aside every couple days, you were doing okay. We were marched around like cattle. We were told when to eat, when to go to the bathroom, when to blink and what to think.

I have never wavered in my support of such a rigid

routine. It built character and perseverance—at least that's what it did for me, and I think it could work the same wonders on almost anybody. We could probably solve a whole mess of problems if we sent our young people off to a place like Parris Island and made them toe the line for eleven weeks. I don't care if they're good kids or bad kids, they would all gain from the experience, and the country would be a better, safer, more productive place to live as a result.

Today I am a loud proponent of some kind of national service program for high school graduates, and my belief goes back to my time at Parris Island. If we can't legislate national service across the board, we can at least incorporate it into government-backed careers and programs. If you want to apply for a government loan, or attend a state school, or accept a civil service appointment, then I believe you should serve your country in just this way, and let your country pay you back with some discipline and direction.

Of course, the regimen would have to be toned down a bit for civilians. In my time, boot camp prepared us to fight. It was drilled into us that anything our superior said was right and anything we said was wrong. In fact, there was no reason for us to say anything at all. We never questioned authority or failed to carry out an order. I was trained to kill without thinking about it and to do what I was supposed to do without thinking about it. By the time I graduated, if my number was called to go to Vietnam, I would have gone and survived. I would have come home.

I was a firm believer in the system, for that time and place, even though our drill instructors occasionally crossed the line. When they did, we had to shoulder it, but it didn't always work that way. One incident nearly got me court-martialed and threw most of what I was taught into question. We had a couple of over-aggressive drill instructors assigned to our unit, the kind of career military guys who sometimes took their authority to extremes. One of their more questionable exercises was to pack forty or fifty of us into the showers, turn the water on hot, pour ammonia and bleach all over the floor and have us do calisthenics.

It was one of those group showers, like they have in a high school locker room, with maybe ten or twelve shower heads; it was big enough for ten or twelve guys, but not forty or fifty, stripped down to our shorts doing push-ups and side straddlehops and mountain climbers. It was unnecessary, and dangerous, but we had to follow orders or risk disciplinary action. Guys were slipping on the wet tile, cracking their heads, stinging their eyes from the ammonia. Over the next few days, when we were out on our morning runs, a lot of us fell out with shortness of breath and a burning sensation in our lungs—all of it due to this cruel business back in the showers.

One guy had a particularly tough time, and he was called in for a dressing-down. I happened to be his platoon guide, which meant that I was called in too, for failing to keep this kid in line. I wasn't supposed to help him or talk to him, but somehow I was expected to motivate him by example. He was, in a way, my responsibility.

When we got to the drill instructor's quarters, I was told to face the wall. Then the drill instructor took a wooden hanger, wrapped it in a towel, and proceeded to beat the crap out of this kid. I watched the whole thing from the corner of my eye, all the time wondering what the hell this beating was meant to accomplish and what I was supposed to do in the face of it. Regrettably, what I was supposed to do was nothing. I was there, in the room, silenced by the unwritten code of the military, my back turned on a painfully degrading act of brutality. There was nothing for me to do but wait it out, and I didn't feel good about it but that's what I did.

A few days later, the kid reported the incident to the chaplain, and he claimed I was in on the beating. This was nonsense—I was a recruit just like him—but I was dragged into it. The kid named me, and I was screwed. I was never charged with any wrongdoing, but I had to account for my presence and tell what I knew.

There was a full-blown investigation, and this was not the time to be involved in a full-blown investigation at Parris Island. In the previous year, Marine Corps officials had been burned by two incidents there (in one, a recruit killed himself by lying down in front of an oncoming train at a nearby railroad crossing; in another, a kid was beaten to death with a pugil stick), and they were out to quash any new controversy before it could reach the papers.

I was asked to testify. Actually, "asked" is probably too soft a word. It's more accurate to say I was forced to testify, or be charged with obstruction, and I was confronted by the most important dilemma of my young life. The Marine Corps lawyers assigned to the case knew I didn't have anything to do with the beating, but they needed me to corroborate this kid's story. I was eighteen years old, away from home for the first time, being asked to serve up a drill instructor who had shown ridiculously poor judgment. It went against everything I stood for, inasmuch as I stood for anything at that age. It also went against everything we were taught in boot camp. Being a Marine was all about honor and pride and integrity. It was about following orders, and the chain of command. It was also about loyalty—to your troops, to your commanding officer, to the United States of America. We would fight for each other and die for each other. We were all in the same foxhole together.

But being a Marine was also about right and wrong, and I knew what this drill instructor had done was wrong. It was beyond the pale, and yet I had no idea what to do about it. My responsibilities were unclear. In the end, my actions were pretty much determined for me, but I wrestled with them just the same. At first I tried to stonewall the lawyers' questions. I didn't lie, but I left a few things out. My face was to the wall, I said. I couldn't see what was going on. But these guys knew I was being evasive, and eventually I was given a direct order to answer truthfully or be court-martialed. By "truthfully" they meant I was to tell them what they wanted to hear. I should have had my own lawyer present, but I didn't know enough to ask for one. I was a scared kid, and as it was I spent half my time trying not to mess up. I thought if I'd asked for a lawyer, my military life would have been over, and I didn't want my military life to be over.

To me, a direct order was a direct order, so I finally

broke and acknowledged that the incident had taken place as the kid described. The lawyers backed off, but my testimony marked me for the rest of my time at Parris Island. The drill instructor was disciplined and reassigned, and I was branded as the guy who did him in. It didn't matter that it was the kid who reported the beating; I was the one who delivered the damaging testimony; I was the one who put him away.

It was a horrible period for me, and for the first time in my life I questioned my own code of conduct. Understand, I grew up at a time when half the kids in my neighborhood had a brother or a cousin off in Vietnam, and half of that group never came home. I grew up at a time when the civil rights movement was at its fiercest and most proud, when bottles were being thrown through windows, when buildings were being torched. I grew up at a time when you sometimes took the heat for your brother's actions. And in the short time I had to grow up at Parris Island, I was taught to believe that my troops came first, my superiors came first, and that I should stand by the bunch of them and go down with the ship.

I accepted the military code, and here it was being pulled out from under me by the same folks who put it there. The Marine Corps was saying, Forget what we've already told you. Do this one thing for us and then put your loyalty back in place. I wasn't proud of what I did, but I was boxed in. It felt like I had no choice. The lawyers had me thinking either I would go to jail or the drill instructor would go to jail, and I couldn't see why I should take the fall for that jerk. I wanted to hold my tongue, and I tried to hold my tongue, but I didn't like the consequences. They didn't seem fair. I hadn't broken any laws. I hadn't even behaved badly or shown poor judgment. I was simply in the wrong place at the wrong time, and I was being jammed because of it.

Naturally, I was seen as the guy who was doing the jamming, and a lot of the other drill instructors had it out for me the rest of my time there. Even some of the other recruits treated me differently for a time. I understood that. Hell, I was out looking for the kid who took the beating, for turning in my name in the first place. I wanted a piece of him the same way those drill instructors wanted a piece of me.

But I never took it out on this kid. I took it out on myself instead. I had to live with what I had done. I convinced myself that I had merely supplanted my drill instructor with a higher authority, that since he answered to the lawyers and investigators working his case, then I had to answer to them as well. I never fully bought my own arguments, but I came to accept that I had done the only thing I could have done. There was no other way.

Out of all this, I developed my own code, and I've tried to live by it ever since. I am loyal, but not blindly loyal. I stand behind people who stand behind me. I protect myself and my family and my friends. I take responsibility for my own actions, but not necessarily for someone else's. And I try never to betray someone's faith or trust. If you believe in me, I will believe in you; if you screw me over, I will find some way to return the favor.

After boot camp, I went to Twentynine Palms—a

desert warfare training base about eighty miles from Palm Springs, California—where I was assigned to the commanding officer's staff as a troop handler. I'd put in for communications and electronics training, thinking I could at least learn how to put a radio together and build a good background for when I finally got to school, but some of my superiors had a different course in mind. They were impressed by my leadership potential and my record at Parris Island and recommended I apply to the Naval Academy Prep School, in Newport, Rhode Island.

At the time, I had no idea what the prep school was all about or how it had anything to do with a Marine like me, but they explained that I could make a lateral transfer and maintain my enlisted rank during the year it took to prep for admission into the Naval Academy in Annapolis, Maryland. If it turned out I was accepted at Annapolis (and the odds were about ten to one against), I would then be discharged from the Marine Corps and reenlisted as a midshipman.

The more I learned about the Naval Academy, the more appealing it became. It was traditionally ranked as one of the top academic schools in the country, on a par with the Ivy League universities and some of the other more distinguished private institutions. If I was accepted, and completed the course of study, I could accomplish my objectives in double time. Rather than serve out my four-year enlisted tour and then enroll in a four-year college on the G.I. Bill, I could get an education and fulfill my duties concurrently—all on the government's dime. I'd owe another five years of service after graduation, but I'd have a guaranteed job at a decent salary. I was already considering a military career, so it was almost like getting something for nothing.

It sounded like a good deal to me, so I applied, becoming the first black enlisted Marine to go to the Naval Academy Prep School (to later graduate from Annapolis). I don't remember attaching all that much significance to this fact at the time, but it was important enough for someone to point it out to me, so I mention it here. There were forty Marines in a class of about 397, and twenty of us made it through the one-year program. Only eleven of us received appointments to Annapolis, and of that group only four graduated.

Academics aside, Annapolis was no elite private school like Harvard or Yale, where gaining admission was supposedly the hardest part of the program. All of us attended the Naval Academy on the taxpayer's dime, and we were made to earn our education at every step. It was a fairly rigorous curriculum, designed to weed out the folks who couldn't cut it. The course work and the long hours in class were demanding enough, but on top of all that we had to train for our PFTs—the physical fitness tests we had to take every semester—and adhere to the usual constraints of a military life.

I struggled throughout my four years at Annapolis, but I somehow managed to stay ahead of the curve. I had never really learned how to be a good student, and this was no place to pick up the habit. In high school, I was able to get by without much effort. Here, though, it was all I could do to keep from falling behind. I applied myself, but I was never sure it was in the right ways. I only failed one course at the Naval Academy— a physics class, my first time around—but there was always a point in the middle of each semester when I didn't know if I'd make it.

Being so close to home didn't necessarily make things any easier. The proximity was more curious than anything else. I grew up less than twenty miles from Annapolis, and I never really knew what went on there. In high school, I ran with a group of guys who went out looking for the midshipmen in town on leave, looking for trouble, and now I was on the other side of those taunts and stares. All of a sudden, I was one of those funny-looking guys in the funny-looking white uniforms, and I didn't know what to think of myself. I was even spat on once or twice, when I was doing the town in my uniform. When I was in boot camp, we were still at the tail end of an unpopular war, and now that I was at Annapolis, there was a lingering resentment toward any symbol of American military involvement in Vietnam. When I went home on leave, I was that symbol to all the kids in my neighborhood, and it was tough to try and see myself through their eyes.

It was all part of a profound personal change. I recharged my faith in God and country. I learned how to box. I studied Chinese. I shaved my head—which everyone thought was far more eccentric than the regulation crew cut, but which I thought was just easier to maintain. I ran myself into the best shape of my life.

And I beat the odds and stayed with the program. I hit the books like no one else I knew. I watched my fellow Marines fall, one by one, but I hung in there. I challenged myself and refused to fail. I was never a gifted student, but I made myself into a tough one. There was no denying me.

It was the most challenging period of my life, but I was never satisfied with the way I met the call. Oh, I met it, but I didn't meet it fully. Underneath my passing grades there was always the gnawing sense that I could be doing more, that I could apply myself better, work harder, be a little more enterprising in my study habits. Getting by may have cut it in high school, but it was no longer enough, and even as my passing grades improved I couldn't shake thinking I was letting myself down, selling myself short.

When I graduated, it should have been the proudest day of my life—but to me it was only a hollow accomplishment. Scratch me and I would have bled with the opportunities missed, the time wasted, the moments lost to uncertainty, immaturity, arrogance, sloth.

Even today, I look back on my time at the Naval Academy with mixed emotions. I was blessed to have been there at all, but cursed for not making the best of it, for not demanding the best of myself.

I should have moved mountains to get through the academy, but instead I found a place to rest just below the summit. It was enough to let me pass to the next phase of my military career, but it wasn't enough for me.

4

I Love It When a Plan Comes Together

After graduating from Annapolis, I became a special duty intelligence officer (cryptologic officer). My first duty assignment after Annapolis was on Guam. For a kid who'd only been on an airplane once before enlisting in the Marine Corps, I was suddenly a world removed from anything I had ever known. At times, it felt like someone had plucked me from my uncertain childhood in Baltimore and dropped me in the middle of nowhere, expecting me to do a man's job; at other times, if felt like I was ready for anything and that the chain of decisions that led me to Guam were made with a clear purpose; most times, I was caught somewhere in between.

I could have pursued a number of fields, drawing on my Naval Academy education, but my interests in language, engineering and technology took me here. Cryptology is the exploitation of radio and electromagnetic spectrum waves, which for military purposes (and mine) meant the intercepting and interpretation of various communications transmissions.

I was stationed on Guam for about a year and a half, but I was only on the island for nine months. The rest of the time I was at sea. I was on island long enough to get married—somewhat in haste and for all the wrong reasons. I must tread lightly around this subject, in order to protect this woman's privacy (we are no longer together), but there is no avoiding the emotions surrounding this stage in my life. Those were mine, and they belong in this account.

The early years of my marriage were an important, defining period for me, probably the first critical juncture in my young life, and I have struggled to understand them ever since. It's clear to me I made some mistakes, but it's not clear what all of them were. I think the biggest mistake, in retrospect, was that I was a little too open to the idea of marriage, probably because of the routine I'd fallen into once I left Annapolis.

As a sailor, we sometimes spent one hundred days straight at sea, and the first two things we used to do when we got off a ship were get a drink and find a woman. I'm not particularly proud of my carousing, and I don't set this out to boast, but I think it's important to explain how things were for me at the time. I was always pulling into one port or another and hopping into bed with one local woman or another, and it wasn't long before the novelty wore off. The women I met were much more forward than the women I had known, and they had a lot less to say. I was as red-blooded as the next guy on board, but I was getting to the point where I wanted something more than a casual physical relationship from the women in my life.

Finally, back on Guam, I found someone I thought I could talk to. She was also in the military, stationed there, and I saw in her the chance to settle down. There was a strong physical attraction, but I think I willed something more into the relationship. Still, I was too young and unsure of myself to be married, even if the contrast to the way I'd been living seemed quiet and comforting. I was too young emotionally and too young professionally. I had no idea where my career would take me, and it was foolish to intertwine another unpredictable military life with mine.

But it was a mistake I was determined to make, and I made it big-time. The marriage lasted nine years, yet I knew it was over after about a month. We stayed together long enough to produce two beautiful daughters, Ashley and Maressa, and for them I am truly grateful, but in every other respect the relationship was a disaster. We drifted apart as quickly as we came together. Just a few weeks after we were married in 1982, I was transferred to Monterey, California, to study Russian for a year at the Defense Language Institute there. After that, my wife and I were together only on and off—on enough to start and sustain a family, and off enough to reinforce that we really weren't meant to be together.

Our time apart began to have less and less to do with each other. In the fifty-two weeks I was in Monterey, I came to realize how little we had in common, beyond the U.S. Navy. We saw each other a couple times over the course of that year, on leave, and during these visits I'd try to find some middle ground on which we might get together. It never even occurred to me at this point that marriage was anything but a lifetime commitment, so I was pretty diligent about trying to work things out.

As it happened, my career kept us apart more often than not. After I completed my degree in Russian, I was reassigned to the National Security Agency and stationed at Fort Meade, Maryland. The Army guys at the Defense Language Institute all went off to work as military attachés, but naval officers like myself tended to go back to sea, so that's what I did. Back then, black naval officers were typically assigned to fields other than cryptology, but by now cryptology was what I wanted and what I knew. Up until about twelve years earlier, you couldn't find a black cryptologic officer anywhere in the U.S. Navy. Despite all our advances on the civil rights front, and despite lip service to the contrary from military higher-ups, blacks were not given the security clearances necessary to do the job. Now that some of these antediluvian prejudices were finally beginning to fade, I wanted to see if I could break some new ground and move some of these old mountains from my path.

(Understand, I am inhibited by certain security constraints surrounding my military career, so in the next few pages I will offer just the broad strokes of what I was doing and where I was doing it. I wouldn't want to compromise national security interests just for the sake of selling a few books; I'll leave that to Tom Clancy.)

My first mission was on a surface ship in and around Central America just before the attack on Grenada. We were back in a foreign port at the time of the invasion, but we were one of the first ships to arrive on the scene the day after the initial engagement, providing support to the invasion team.

After Grenada, I began a three-year tour of submarine duty, during which I spent a little less than half my time underwater, chiefly on three separate missions. At sea, I was in charge of a group of ten to fifteen enlisted cryptologic technicians in the Direct Support Division, and we spent a lot of our time on dry land prepping and debriefing and vying for our next assignments. In between, there were routine workups and certification runs on the subs, and various surface-ship deployments that kept me away from home for weeks at a stretch. I was in and out of port constantly while my wife was pregnant with our first child, so this was something of an uneasy period for me. In fact, I was out on an orientation trip for my first submarine mission in the weeks leading directly up to our due date.

The work was exciting, but I was pulled by what was going on at home. Obviously, these missions were port-to-port operations. We closed the hatch and sailed off. There was no turning back for any reason—certainly not for the birth of Lieutenant William's first child. There was also no direct contact with your family while you were at sea. For longer missions, we could each receive one thirty word telegram every two weeks or so; for shorter hauls such as this, there was no communication at all.

Every night I prayed we would make it back in time for the baby, and we did. Ashley was born about a week late—on March 21, 1985—and I got to spend two weeks with her before I shipped out again. Actually, to call it two weeks is generous. We spent just an hour or two a day together for the next ten or twelve days. Even when I was back at the base, I logged long hours prepping for our next mission, so my time with the baby was carefully measured. I took her out of her crib in the middle of the night, if that was the only time we had. I figured I could sleep the following year, and she could make it up in the morning.

My early experiences with Ashley reinforce my belief that there are no good excuses for working parents to miss out on their children. Oh, there are plenty of excuses, but none of them are any good. I don't care what you do for a living, or how crazy-making your hours happen to be, there is always a way to carve out some time to spend with your child. As long as you live in the same house, you can work something out. Wake the child up in the middle of the night if you have to, as I had to. It's not the preferred course, I know, but you've got to take what you can get.

I was nowhere near prepared for the sheer joy of being a father. When I was alone with Ashley, in the middle of the night, I'd tell her all kinds of things. She was asleep or crying, but I ran my mouth off. I told her all the things I hoped to do in this world and all the things I hoped for her. I wanted to make her proud, just as she filled me with pride every time I held her. I wanted to give her the kind of storybook growing-up that my parents had been unable to give me.

Some of these stolen, late-night sessions were bitter-sweet. As I'd gaze at Ashley's sleeping face, I sometimes wondered how any parent could raise a hand to their children. She looked so peaceful, so helpless, so completely dependent. I never truly understood my father's outbursts, but now that I was a parent, it was unfathomable to me. It was beyond understanding. I just had to accept it if I ever hoped to achieve any kind of adult relationship with him, and move on from there.

These moments were bittersweet, also, because I knew they were only fleeting. In just a few days, I would be shipping out again, and after another stretch of carefully measured time with Ashley there'd be some other mission to pull me away. On top of that, there was all this uncertainty surrounding my marriage, and I couldn't shake thinking that my little girl had been dealt a lousy hand. Either her father would be off at sea, sometimes for as long as three months, or floundering in his relationship with her mother at home, which put me at sea in a figurative sense as well. The poor kid couldn't tell if I was coming or going or staying—and neither could I.

Let me slip in a word or two on submarine life, before I go any further, because the routine did more than pull me from my baby daughter; it also did as much to shape me during this period as my new role of parent did. First of all, submarine life is not something you can jump into with both feet. We were kind of eased into it with a five-day workup, and then an eight-day workup, but even these mini-tours were difficult. I'd stepped aboard a sub many times before I submerged in one, and the difference was everything. Underwater, for any stretch of time, a submarine becomes an eerie, claustrophobic environment, and I was scared to death during my first workup. It was almost like a phobia. Even knowing we would surface in just a few days, I was in a near panic. I eventually got used to it, but not in time for my first real mission. I honestly thought I would leave fingernail marks down the pier when the ship pulled away.

On a submarine, there is no morning, noon or night. Everything is dark. There is usually just one periscope, and only three or four people get to look through it, so there is no sunlight except by report. There is no sense of time beyond the twenty-four-hour military clock. You know where you have to be and when you have to be there, and that you'd better catch your sleep when you can. We worked in shifts, and they were what broke up your days.

The most disconcerting adjustment was in never having to focus your eyes on an object any greater than thirty feet away. That's about the furthest distance your eyes would travel before something—a wall or a door— would break your line of vision. Everything gets to look a little hazy after a while on such close inspection.

The sleeping quarters were extremely confining and accounted for much of the eerie claustrophobia. As an officer, I had it a bit better than most, but this wasn't saying much. I shared a miniature stateroom with the executive officer, although "miniature stateroom" was a grand term: it was no bigger than a small powder room, with two bunks and a small desk. Everything folded into the wall, so that if we weren't using one piece of furniture, we could make room for another. There was maybe one spot in the entire room where you could stretch your arms out completely without hitting a wall.

The enlisted men "hot-racked" in bunks stacked four high. ("Hot-racking" meant the bunks were used constantly, by shifts.) There was probably no more than two feet of head room separating the top of the bunk from the bottom of the other. If you wanted to switch from sleeping on your stomach to sleeping on your back, you had to climb out and back in again. There was no turning over.

You ended up living for meals. I did, anyway. We had a meal at six in the morning, another at noon, and another at six in the evening, and these only loosely resembled breakfast, lunch and dinner. Without a sense of night and day, our bodies adjusted to an all-purpose diet. There was also a midnight meal—"midrats"—for those of us on the late shift. For me, the chief attraction of the meal was not the food itself, but the chance to visit the most spacious room on ship and to visit with such a large group all at once. Mealtime offered the only real sense of community we had at sea. At all other times, it was like being in a vacuum.

About the only other release available to us was a makeshift weight room I was able to organize with the help of our commanding officer. I paid for most of the equipment out of my own pocket, but the commanding officer on my first ship made it possible. He didn't have to give us the space, but he did, and after that it was easier to convince my subsequent C.O.s to do the same. There was only enough room for one of us to work out at a time, and we had to be extremely careful laying the barbells down on the steel floor (if we dropped one, the boat would thunder with the noise, thereby stripping the submarine of its greatest asset—silence—and leaving our mission vulnerable), but it was a great way to let off steam and stay in shape. I don't know what some of the guys would have done without it, myself included.

As for the work itself, it was exciting and nervous-making as hell. I'd never known anything like it. This was where the rubber met the road, although that's probably not the best metaphor if you're in the middle of the ocean. In a time of peace, this was as close to a warlike situation that we could possibly find ourselves in, and it was thrilling. I never had a death wish, or anything like that, but I loved to be challenged, and this was the biggest test of all.

In many ways, I was directly responsible for the lives of the 120 people on board. Obviously, the ultimate responsibility rested with the captain, but as the cryptologic officer I was the one he relied on to be his eyes and ears regarding enemy activity. The success of our missions and the safety of our crew rested on my ability to remain alert and focused.

I was never more anxious than the first time we closed the hatch and shipped out for a three-month stretch. It was more than simple panic. It was something else. I felt it the second and third times too, and the feelings stayed with me until each mission was completed. I've never known that feeling again, in quite the same way. For most of the crew, when that hatch closed, their lives were on the line. For me, it was my life *and* my ass, and this made a big difference. My whole career hinged on whatever was to happen over the next eighty or ninety days. Even if we survived one of my miscalculations, I was still toast. I'd be out of the service as soon as they could open the hatch and get rid of me.

It was an awesome responsibility, and I believe I shouldered it well. If I made a marginally bad call once, I never made it again, and by my second or third mission even the smallest bad calls were a memory. Usually, the captain acted on my recommendations, so I clearly had to know my stuff. To be honest, I was never really worried about my abilities, but I was concerned about staying vigilant and on top of things over some of my longer shifts. The pressure was enormous and intense, and the working conditions somewhat less than desirable, but I always rose to the occasion.

Adrenaline can do funny things to a person's judgment, but fortunately it sharpened mine. Sometimes, to kind of rally myself to the task when I was pumped full of adrenaline without a clear path in mind, I repeated a line from The A-Team, one of the popular television shows at the time. At the end of each episode, George Peppard used to say, "I love it when a plan comes together." That was what it was like for me on almost every shift. I studied. I looked. I listened. I processed volumes of information and applied what I knew to the changing situation. And then I rocked—drawing on everything I'd learned to make a sure recommendation.

I loved it when a plan came together—and somehow one always did. The seat of my pants invariably took me where I had to go.

By my second mission, I was an old hand. I hated the idea of being separated from Ashley for three months, but there was a part of me that now longed to ship back out. As much as I dreaded my first mission, I wanted another chance to close the hatch and get back to it. I found myself missing everything I complained about on the first pass—the claustrophobia, the lingering weirdness of not knowing whether it was night or day. Everything was tugging at me, pulling me back to sea: the camaraderie, the thrill of doing a job well.

We submarine direct support officers were probably the most arrogant sons of bitches in the cryptologic community. There were only about three dozen of us with the security clearance to know what was actually going on out there, but there was no denying those in the know. We came back with an attitude bigger than Maine; and in some respects that attitude was justified. Some of the junior officers, trying to become qualified, would look at us like we walked on water, and I'll admit we played into that image. I know for myself, if I came back from a successful mission or was cited with a Navy Achievement Medal, Navy Commendation Medal or Meritorious Service Medal, I walked around like hot stuff until my next assignment came around. I was the man, and no one could touch me.

There was a tremendous rush to what we did when we did it well, and once we got it in our blood, we wanted more. There's not a false, euphoria-inducing chemical in this world that could surpass what I tasted down in those subs. There's nothing like it. And it was like any other high in that you had to come down from it at some point. The withdrawals were especially tough because you couldn't talk about it. You couldn't talk to your wife about it unless she had the same security clearance. You couldn't talk to your friends. What ended up happening was we could only talk to each other, so I spent a lot of time in the office at the base. I had to decompress and take the buzz off so I could get back to being a normal person, but by that time we were getting ready to ship out again.

It's easy to lose a sense of yourself in such an insular world. The military model had me believing that what we were doing was all-important—and it *was* all-important—but I had let it become all-consuming as well. I had this super-inflated idea of who I was, and it didn't fit with the kind of husband I wanted to be, the kind of father I wanted to be, or the kind of man I wanted to be. So I vowed to work against all the ego-driven aspects of my job. It was tough, but I thought it was essential. With this in mind, on my second and third missions, I began to devote some of my downtime to a thorough reevaluation of who I was and what I was doing. I still worked out, and lingered in the wardroom, and caught whatever sleep I could, but I spent countless hours working on myself. I had the national interest to protect, but I could no longer ignore my personal interest. I had a baby now, and I had to stop setting aside my problems at home for another day. This was my other day, and I had to face it. Just as I loved it when a plan came together on duty, I desperately needed a plan for the rest of my life.

I looked over my shoulder at all the bad decisions I'd made, to see where this new dilemma might fit. With such amorphous chunks of time to myself, I developed a style of introspection that I still use. I picked a very finite period in my life—say, the fall of 1977—and tried to relive that period in as much detail as I could possibly recall. Some nights, I stayed at it twelve hours straight, peeling away at the layers of my memory until I got at the truth. I looked at relationships I had, and where they went wrong, conversations that didn't turn out the way I had hoped or intended, judgment calls I made that now led me to wonder what the hell I was thinking. I remembered words I wished I could have sucked back in my face and never have said, hurtful things that I did to people that I would never allow myself to do again.

I spent many nights focused on Ashley's mother, trying to see precisely where our relationship might have turned, and if there was any way to turn it back around. I started to think that maybe I couldn't stay married, even though I couldn't stand the thought of not being with Ashley. I was only out at sea a few days before I ached to hold her.

These shift-long introspections were not just directed at improving myself, or saving my marriage, or find-

ing a way to be with my baby girl. I also looked close-
ly at my military career, which by the end of my third
submarine mission was coming to a crossroads. By the
time we pulled back into port, I would have logged five
years of service beyond Annapolis, fulfilling my duty
obligations and freeing me to consider my options. Did
I want to stay on or move on? Where did I belong?
What did I want to do? Could I buy into this puffed-
up sense of self-importance (which I supposed was
necessary to a successful military operation) and still
step off the ship and be a regular human being? Could
I live with a career that kept me away from home more
often than not? What kind of father could I be if I was
never around?

I did some real serious soul-searching on this, and
while a lot of my career concerns were tied to my marriage, a great deal of them stood on their own. I loved
what I was doing, but I didn't like the things my job
was doing to me, the kind of person it was turning me
into. I had my language training, my electronics training, and my engineering degree. There were any number of things I could have done in the private sector—
all of them for a great deal more money than the
$35,000 salary I was pulling down as a naval officer.
Already, I'd been approached by a number of compa-
nies doing business under military or government con-
tracts, with whom I'd come into contact during the
course of my duties. There were jobs out there for me.

But my career wasn't just about money. It was also
about making a difference, pushing myself to new lim-
its. It was about setting difficult but realistic goals. I

started to think I would someday be the first black admiral in the history of U.S. Navy cryptology. It was not out of the realm of possibility if I continued to do my job well. I was probably one of the most highly decorated lieutenants in my job specialty. There was no reason my military career could not take me wherever I wanted to go.

Then again, there was every reason. I couldn't clearly see what was going on back home. It took a long time for me to consider how my wife and daughter were responding to my not being there. Nobody counseled us on the changes our families were going through while we were away. A lot of the guys were facing all kinds of power struggles with their wives. They were off at sea for three months at a time, and their wives had to become more independent in their absence. They had to pay the bills, get the roof fixed, maybe even buy a new car. Children naturally became more attached to the parent who was home with them, and a bit tentative with the parent who was rarely around.

That was the way it was in my house too, I realized. My wife was becoming a different person. I was becoming a different person. We borrowed from each other's roles and developed new ones. Our relationship was changing—and in our case it was not for the better.

As I lay in my bunk trying to puzzle it all together, I made a decision. I could not go on like this. We could not go on like this. As much as I loved my work, it wasn't worth what it was doing to my family. I craved the adrenaline rush of these sub missions, but the cost was too steep. I simply could not afford to let our family dynamic take any further shape without me.

Now all I needed was for a plan to come together.

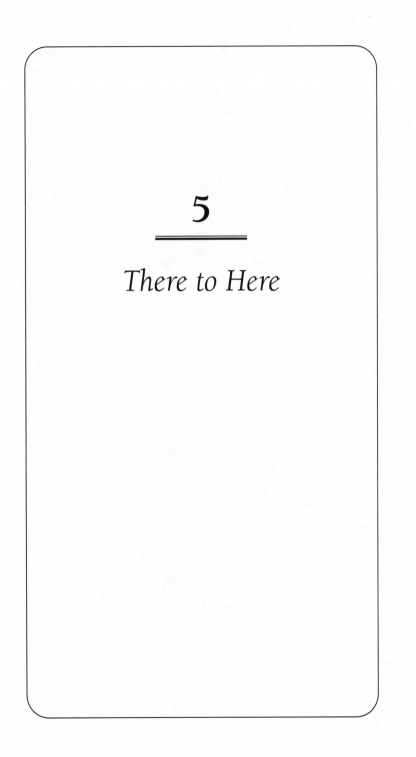

5

There to Here

A plan came together soon enough, even if it took a while to present itself. As a matter of fact, I was off pursuing this whole other course when I just stumbled onto the path that was meant for me.

Just a few weeks after my last sub run, I was offered a post overseeing the submarine cryptologic officers in the Naval Security Group's Fleet Support Division at Fort Meade. It was, I thought at the time, a tremendous opportunity and a possible solution to my problems at home. As an operations officer, I would clearly have to do some traveling, to coordinate the various submarine missions from bases up and down the coast, but I would be stationed at Fort Meade, Maryland, and rarely away from home for more than a couple days. It seemed like a perfect fit, once I was asked to try it on. The job itself didn't promise any significant bump in salary, but the appointment was a powerful validation—that I was doing good work and that my superiors thought I was capable of more of the same.

Some of the private-sector offers I had been considering would have paid as much as $80,000 per year to start, but I couldn't see being on the civilian side of the military equation at this point in my career, even at these prices. Yes, the money was important, but it wasn't everything. It was important because I had started to think about a divorce, and I knew I'd need a little cash cushion to see me through the procedure. But there were other factors. For one thing, the military could never lay me off—unless I really screwed up bigtime, and this wasn't about to happen. When one of these outside companies lost a major military contract, which happened from time to time, a whole mess of people lost their jobs. I couldn't afford to be one of those people, especially if I was in the middle of a divorce proceeding. For another, none of these private-sector jobs promised anything like the responsibility of the ops position. This was the key. I loved the fast track I was riding and craved the responsibility. If I left the military, all I'd be was a well-compensated salesman of technical equipment. Oh, they'd slap me with some important title—like Vice President, Naval Fleet Support Augmentation—but there would be no changing the fact that I was just a salesman. It seemed like the end of the line, and I was too young to sell out just yet.

At Fort Meade, I was directly responsible for a $1–$5-million budget and millions of dollars worth of equipment. There were about a hundred people reporting to me. Now there was a whole new mountain range to climb, and each peak was its own drug. I was like a junkie, desperate for a fix, and I found it each day, in one form or another. When I was learning the job, the fix came in figuring new approaches to old problems or in mastering some bureaucratic nuance or motivating the troops. When I was up and running, it was in hitting my stride and making a difference. Always, at the end of each day, I could point to something I had done to make myself proud and look ahead to some other thing I might do tomorrow.

I was a whole lot less sure of myself at home. I was busy with all kinds of lawyers, seeing about filing divorce papers, but for some reason I couldn't pull the trigger. These days, when I'm doing a show or giving one of my talks, I'm usually pretty hard on couples who can't quite get their act together about obtaining a divorce and moving on with their lives, but I'm really not one to talk. I dragged my feet like most everyone else. (Hell, we weren't ever separated!) Either I was concerned about the money, or intimidated by the paperwork, or unsure of how it would all affect Ashley. I was working like a demon over at the base and doing some traveling, so I wasn't home all that much, and when I was away from home, I sometimes thought the problems would take care of themselves. It was a selfish, do-nothing approach, and I made it a lot tougher on all of us than it really had to be, but there it was.

The irony to all of this was that it was around this time that I took a new job—with a special, high-level operation known as Classic Paladin—during which I started to counsel some of my men and their wives on the problems they were having in their own marriages. Who was I to talk, right? But that's just what I did, and it was a good thing too. Like I said before, none of the brass paid any real attention to the domestic problems of the troops, and now that some of these guys were reporting to me, I thought I could do something about it. At least I could try. It was like that old saying we used to kick around in high school: Those who can't do, teach. Well, I couldn't do anything about my own situation, but maybe I could get some of these folks to avoid some of my same mistakes.

This extra effort had nothing official to do with my new job, but I thought it had everything to do with it. After all, it made sense to me that if all was right on the home front, my men would work with clearer heads when they were out at sea. I was convinced that even a one-day problem at home would translate to a one-day problem on the job. You can line up all the psychologists in the world to tell me that there are some people who can separate the two and live a kind of double life, but I just don't buy it. And when it comes to a job like ours, where you're in a life-and-death situation and half a world away, then the state of mind of your troops is especially important. I had guys out at sea for stretches as long as 170 days, and then I'd bring them home for three months and prep them to go back out again. This was their whole existence, and a lot of them were neglecting their wives and their children. I had men in my command who came home to babies they had never seen or to wives who couldn't stand the loneliness and had taken up with someone else. Most of the problems were easily solved—there was one young bride who didn't know how to get her husband's per diem pay started in his absence, and another woman who complained that her husband never wrote to her from overseas—and all it usually took was time and attention to get to the bottom of whatever it was.

I even had my chief petty officer set up a system where we watchdogged our men and made sure they wrote at least one letter home each week. It sounds like childish, hand-holding stuff, I know, but I thought it was important for morale. It's easy to lose track of time at sea and difficult to hold on to whatever was going on back home—and my guys clearly needed a push. At first, a lot of them were ripshit that I was bugging in their business like this, but after a while most came to appreciate it. Mostly, they were grateful that their constant letters had kept them out of hot water.

What began as a kind of informal trouble-shooting effort gradually grew into something more. I started holding meetings every other week in the recreation center at the base, where the wives could show up and work through some of their problems in a group setting. Sometimes I conducted lectures and tried to explain to these women in a nonclassified way why their husbands were overseas for five or six months at a stretch. When my men were home between tours, I made their attendance at these sessions mandatory, and

we did some *informal* family counseling. I can't stress
the informality of these sessions enough. I knew I
wasn't at all qualified to be leading a group like this,
at least not from a social services standpoint, but I
cared, and to me this was qualification enough.
Nobody else cared, and I told myself that what we
were doing had to be better than nothing.

Probably the most important result of these group
sessions, other than the peace of mind my men took
with them back to sea, was that a lot of the wives began
to feel a part of the military community. In the group,
they found a connection. These women came from all
over the country, from all walks of life, but these week-
ly meetings brought them together in ways that mere
proximity and shared circumstance could not. Some of
them formed great friendships with each other, and in
these friendships was the basis for an even stronger
link with their husbands overseas.

Meanwhile, at home, I certainly wasn't practicing
what I was preaching. Our comings and goings sometimes made me think my wife and I were working separate shifts. We did our best to keep out of each other's
way. We found all kinds of creative (and destructive)
ways to run our household without running into each
other. We parented on a kind of tag-team basis, never
together, and I hated what this was doing to Ashley.
Actually, I had no idea what this was doing to Ashley,
but I hated it just the same.

It's funny, and tragic I suppose, but it is only now, in
looking back at this period in my life, that I realize how
royally I messed up. At the time, in the middle of it, I
was so focused on the day-to-day that I never really

looked at the bigger picture, at what all of this pro-
tracted uncertainty was doing to Ashley. I knew her
mother and I had to get a divorce eventually, but I was
deathly afraid of taking that step. That's where we were
headed, but it seemed neither one of us was in any
great rush to get there. For my part, I thought that if I
could just keep on from one day to the next, things
would be okay, but in retrospect that was probably the
worst thing I could have done.

The contrast between my uncertainty at home and
my certainty at the base was astonishing. I was promoted virtually every time I set my sights on a new job.
Within three years, I went from being the guy who
rode the subs, to being the guy who assigned the other
officers to ride the subs, to being the guy in charge of
the Classic Paladin operation, to finally being the guy
on the staff of the commander in chief of the entire
Atlantic Fleet, responsible for all submarine-related
cryptologic assets (equipment and personnel) on the
East Coast.

It was January 1987, and I thought I could see my
life spread out before me. I would finally break with
Ashley's mother. I would be stationed in Norfolk,
Virginia, for at least my next two three-year tours of
duty and continue on this dizzying progression up the
chain of command. I would accomplish great things in
my military career. There would be no looking back.

The Norfolk post was the beginning of a remarkable
tour of duty and a profound change in my personal
life. The one followed from the other. The job required
that I ship back out to sea from time to time, on five-
or six-day trial runs, and I loved being back on a sub-

marine, even for such short intervals. I bounced from one ship to the next, inspecting the work, checking the equipment, evaluating the troops. I had to make sure the cryptologic crews were ready for their missions and that the vendors who serviced and provided the equipment were doing their jobs. And I had to coordinate with the other officers assigned to each sub. It was what I called an incentive job, which to me meant there was a lot riding on every decision I had to make. If I missed a call, the ramifications could have been enormous, so I made damn sure I never missed a call.

In almost every respect it was the perfect appointment, and I couldn't imagine doing anything else. This was where I was meant to be—or so I thought, until I was turned on to something completely different. It happened almost by accident. About nine months into my Norfolk gig, I took a call from an old Naval Academy roommate who was putting together a conference at Kansas State University. His name was Wickliff Paul III, and he was one of the good guys. Wick was organizing something called a MORE (Minority Officer Recruiting Effort) team visit, and he wanted me to come down to Kansas and help out. Back when I was at Fort Meade, I had told him what I was doing with the family support groups, and he thought maybe there was some way to play off of that and develop a related presentation.

I wasn't crazy about the idea. I had never recruited for the military. I thought the choice of going into the service was a very, very private thing. I still feel this way. There is something distasteful to me about trying to convince a young adult to pledge his or her life to the military. Either it's something they feel for themselves, or it isn't. Plus, every single recruiter I'd encountered was a bald-faced liar. They told kids whatever they had to in order to get them to sign up.

As much as I wanted to help out an old buddy, I wasn't about to snow these college students or make any kind of hard sell. But Wick wouldn't let me off the hook. He'd been having all kinds of trouble getting officers to volunteer for the program, so we finally hit on the idea of some kind of leadership seminar that I could moderate, as long as I wouldn't have to stand around afterward and get kids to sign up. I would do my thing, whatever it was, and leave the recruiting aspects to someone else.

Unfortunately, Wick hadn't left me much time to prepare, and I flew out to the Kansas State appearance without any clear idea of what I would say. I hadn't slept in three days, working to clear my docket just so I could make the trip. There had been no time to even think about my presentation, and now that I had the time, I still didn't have a clue. I would have to wing it and see what happened. I knew that if I got rolling on the subjects of leadership and responsibility, I should fill the hour that Wick had set aside for my talk. If I ran out of things to say, I could always throw it open to questions and kill the remaining time.

It wasn't exactly the way I liked to go into a new situation—I prefer to be prepared, and eliminate as much uncertainty as possible—but I hadn't left myself room for anything else. When you don't have anything else to go with, you go with what you have.

What I thought would be a one-shot deal turned

into a brand-new career—virtually overnight. The first seminar I did, at Kansas State, went so well that I was asked to conduct another, later that afternoon, along with a Navy pilot named Drew Brown. The next day, they sent the two of us out to the University of Kansas and to a conference of local school boards, which led to two other invitations to speak at area high schools the following day. Each talk was better attended than the one before, and by the time it was all over we were fielding requests from more high schools than I could accommodate on my four-day leave.

This wasn't quite what my friend Wick had in mind, but it was something. Actually, it was better than something. It was a small wonder.

I really can't explain my reception or my performance. I guess I tapped a vein that needed to be let. I spoke about leadership and responsibility. I spoke about drug abuse and education. I spoke about getting ahead and staying on top. I spoke about wasted time and missed opportunities. My goal was not to win these kids over into thinking about a career in the military. I didn't care at all about that. What I wanted was to get them thinking about their lives beyond school, about issues bigger than themselves. If there were things in my talk that happened to spark an interest in the military, then that would be gravy.

Judging from the questions I took afterward, a lot of these kids were already thinking about the service before I stepped to the podium. They wanted to know if I thought my high school education prepared me for my military career. They wanted to know if there was racism in the military. They wanted to know if enlisting would wash away some of the hard problems they were facing at home.

I gave it to them straight: no, my high school education didn't adequately prepare me for anything; yes, the United States armed forces are as racist as any other organization or segment of our society; no, the only way to deal with your problems is to face them head-on.

The first high school presentation I made rocked me like nothing before in my entire life. The college talks were just enough to get my engine going, but I didn't kick into high gear until I did my thing for the younger kids. And when I did, it was like a brick hit me square on the head and knocked me flat. It left me a different person. I woke up in that auditorium, on a stage in front of one thousand kids, knowing that this was what I was meant to do.

Man, I worked that room like it was my own, like I had been doing it my entire life. I looked out at this sea of vulnerable faces—black, white, Hispanic, Asian, you name it—and what I was saying was registering on each and every one of them. They were hard, but I could actually see them softening. It was incredible. These were supposedly rowdy kids (their teachers told me to keep it short, because they could never keep them quiet for more than five or ten minutes), but I had their complete attention. Most of these kids had spent their entire lives building these rough, impenetrable exteriors, but I saw right through them and they killed the charade straightaway. They hung on every word. And in their eyes, I could see them saying, "Tell me more. Tell me more."

I wish I could remember what I said, but I know how I opened. I stood at the back of the room, in uniform, and from the shadows barked out my credo: "Mountain, get out of my way!" I shouted with everything I had, and these kids quieted down like I had pulled the plug on them. Then I marched down the aisle to the stage and started riffing on whatever came into my head. It's the same way I jump-started every presentation from that day forward—and this was the first of thousands. I had no script, no cue cards, and no idea where I was headed, but something took me to the right place.

I locked into this strange zone, and I could do no wrong. I ripped into these kids for their attitudes, for their willingness to ditch their educations for a good time, for disrespecting their parents, their teachers and each other. No matter what I would say to put these kids down, they'd applaud. I challenged them to take a look at themselves, and they responded like I never would have believed. Really, if I had thought through what I was about to say, I would have talked myself into some other approach. I would have been more conservative, less confrontational, and I probably would have put these kids to sleep.

This way, just going with my gut, I had somehow managed to reach them with authority without sounding like an authority figure.

I was in their faces, and there was no denying me.

When it was over, I was exhilarated—and exhausted. The kids jumped to their feet to give me a standing ovation. I couldn't believe it. I had absolutely no frame of reference for this kind of response. I had never in my life signed an autograph for anybody, and here I was dealing with a line of a couple hundred kids, waiting for me to put my name on a piece of paper. There was pushing and shoving. The principal grabbed a bullhorn to try and quiet everyone down, but this just riled them up even more.

I signed my last autograph and went back to my motel room, spent and uncertain. I was completely wiped out, and completely confused. Everything I knew was turned upside down, and I tried to understand it. I was well along on my career path of U.S. Navy cryptology, but after just these few days it felt like I had made a wrong turn. Suddenly, my dingy hotel room started to feel suffocating and small, and I wanted to get out and go someplace. It almost didn't matter where, just as long as I could put the weirdness of that afternoon on some shelf and not have to think about it.

It was the last day of the conference at the university, so I went back to hear a gospel performance by choirs from all of the participating colleges. In retrospect, I probably went looking to find a minister, someone to talk to who might help me put the weekend's events into some kind of perspective. I probably would have gone to church to pray, but I didn't have a car or know my way around, so this was where I ended up, and as I lost myself in the glorious music I felt my life being ripped away from me and transformed.

It was a palpable, physical thing. Something had happened, and I struggled to make sense of it. What the hell was going on? I was no Michael Jackson. I was no Michael Jordan. I wasn't even Michael Dukakis. I was not singing or dancing or playing hoops or running for President. I wasn't even preaching. In fact, whatever messages I was sending out were undermined by the messages I was living. Look at me! Who was I to try to tell these kids how to live? I couldn't even get off my ass and get a divorce, even when my failure to do so was slowly destroying my wife and my child and myself. Damn, I was still sleeping on my couch!

And yet I must have said *something* right, for all these kids to have responded the way they did. Something must have happened up there on that stage, but what? And what in the world was I going to do about it?

6

Word of Mouth

I was swallowed up by the momentum and dropped back into my routine a different person. In fact, I was so thoroughly recast by the trip to Kansas that my routine could no longer accommodate me.

The changes were a few months in taking shape, but the makeover seemed immediate and inevitable. Here's what happened. There were several influential people at the Kansas conference, and some were so blown away by our presentations that they came up to Drew Brown and myself afterward and invited us to speak at schools in their home state. I loved being complimented as much as the next guy, but underneath the stroking was the muddling thought that my motivational speaking career would not end here. If these back slaps were any measure, I'd be doing this for a long time to come.

At first, I couldn't understand what all the fuss was about, but it makes sense to me now that I've put it in context. We were both black, both articulate, both officers in the U.S. Navy, both good role models for struggling inner-city kids. But it was more than that. Nobody else was out there on the circuit doing what we were doing—speaking to kids in language they could understand, challenging them to make something of their lives—and these folks were anxious to tap into what we apparently had to offer. Remember, this was January 1988, First Lady Nancy Reagan had just started her "Just Say No!" campaign, and the topics of shiftless teenagers and rampant drug abuse were very much on the minds of civic leaders around the country.

When we turned up and these good people heard us speak, they sought to put us to good use. One of these civic-minded folks was a guy named Les Franklin, from the governor's job-training office in Colorado, and he was impressed by one of our talks. I later learned that Les had taken a leave from his senior executive position at IBM to work in Governor Roy Romer's administration and that he was an impressive guy in his own right. He introduced himself after one of our presentations.

"You were wonderful," he said, pumping my hand. "I had no idea the military even had a program like this."

"What program is that?" I wondered. Really, I had no idea.

"This," he said. "You. Getting kids to stay in school and stay straight."

I looked down at my uniform and realized where he was coming from. Les just figured that since I was here, in officer's garb, speaking at what was ostensibly a recruiting seminar, then it must have been part of a sanctioned, institutionalized effort.

"There's no program, sir," I explained. "It's just me, talking to some kids and helping out a friend." I told him how my Annapolis roommate had set up the conference and needed people to round out his schedule.

Les was shocked to learn that this had been an impromptu presentation, but he invited us out to Denver to speak to high school kids there. He didn't care if it was an authorized military program or not; he just wanted in. "You've got a gift, Lieutenant," he said. "Your superiors might be too stupid to take advantage of it, but these kids need to hear from guys like you two."

I flew back to Norfolk, promising to consider his invitation, and when I arrived at the base, I filled my commanding officer in on what had happened. I brought with me a file full of press clippings and letters of appreciation to show him how I was received. There was even a letter from the head of the recruiting command for the Kansas district, thanking me for my efforts and praising my C.O. for making me available to such a worthy cause.

I had more ideas stewing in my head than I knew

what to do with, but one thing was certain: I had to find a way to bounce off of these first few public appearances and build on them. My boss was very obliging and told me I could schedule as many talks as I wanted, provided I worked them around my principal duties. The deal was that as long as I got my job done, the rest would be up to me. I had a considerable amount of leave time coming, so we agreed I would have to charge my time away against that, unless I could find someone to write me a set of orders. (If I was dispatched on official military business, my accumulated leave time would remain untouched.) And, of course, I would have to travel on my own dime; the military wasn't about to pay my way on such a dubious enterprise.

And so I got on the phone with Drew Brown and Les Franklin and scheduled a round of Denver appearances for a few weeks away. I was jazzed, and anxious to be let out of the gate. My work in Norfolk, which had been everything to me just a short time earlier, had become almost drudgery. For the first time in my military career, I felt like I was punching a clock. Some days, I had to check my watch to see that it was working, that's how slow the time was crawling.

I marked the Denver dates on my calendar and drove myself crazy waiting for them to come around. Then I filled some of the in-between time with quick-hit appearances in my home area. This speaking thing had seeped into my blood and I was hooked, so I found my fixes where I could. I don't like to keep falling back on this drug-addiction analogy, but it's the best way I can think to describe what I was going through. There was a real adrenaline high to those first few appearances, and now that I'd sampled the feeling, I wanted more. It was the closest thing I'd found to match the emotional rush at the end of a successful sub run, and this one only took an hour or two to achieve. It was like an instant buzz—just add water and stir— and when I came down from one, I could just drive to the next town and get started on another.

No question about it, I was addicted.

I drove out to Virginia Beach to make a presentation at a hospital, and arranged for another talk at a local high school as long as I was there. It was a predominantly white school district, but it didn't make any difference. The same messages applied, and I delivered them in the same ways. These kids were screaming from the rafters by the time I was through, and underneath the shouts I wondered what it was, precisely, that kept pulling such a response. Were young people in America so desperate for direction that they would suck up whatever came close? Had their parents and teachers really checked out and left these kids to figure things through for themselves? Were they all so rootless and hopeless that they'd put their sorry asses in the hands of someone like me?

Back in Norfolk, I started calling everyone I knew who might have some connection to area school boards or youth groups. I was eager to tap into the local high schools, to try out my new calling. My father was by this point the commissioner of Public Works in Baltimore, and he set up a meeting with the school board president so I could make my pitch there. Dad had no idea what I was up to, or why I would set aside my work in cryptology, but he made the arrangements just the same. Before I knew it I was driving up to Baltimore with Drew Brown, staying in my parent's house, and visiting four or five high schools in the space of two days.

Each time out, I was lifted up and let loose. I was soaring, and rocking, and giving these screaming kids the lesson of their lives. I had no idea what had come over me, but I gave myself over to it completely.

The trip out to Denver was everything I'd hoped and like nothing I'd imagined. Les Franklin set me up at a half dozen schools—one for pregnant girls, one for troubled youths, and so on—and I went into each like all our lives depended on it. I truly felt that I was the last and best shot some of these kids would ever have. If I couldn't reach them, they'd be gone, so I dug deep and hit my mark. It felt great, marching down those aisles, shouting out my message ("Mountain, get out of my way!"), stepping up on stage and giving everything I had.

By this time, I had hit a kind of groove, and I was starting to figure which riffs would work and which would fall flat. I still didn't speak from notes, but if something worked in Kansas City or Virginia Beach, then I trotted it out again in Denver. I started to polish my act (and it was, in almost every sense, a performance) and shed some of my attitude. I thought of my presentation as a kind of emotional roller coaster, with dips and climbs, low spots and highs, and I was out to take these kids on an incredible ride. I tried to keep my focus narrow and my points clear. I was learning that the surest way to lose an audience was to beat them over the head with the same lesson, over and over, so I made sure to beat them over the head with a whole bunch of lessons, over and over. And I'd never let up until what I was saying had sunk all the way in.

After Denver, we were hit with seventy or eighty requests from high schools all over the country, and I worried how I would meet the call and still stay on top of my job. This was the beginning of an extremely spiritual time in my life. I prayed long and hard about what I should do. I had been on an extremely fast track, and I was young enough and decorated enough to have accomplished great things in my military career, but all of this seemed suddenly small against what I might accomplish with these high school kids. In my prayers and in my heart, I realized that this speaking thing was what I was put on this planet to do. Nothing else mattered. God had given me a talent—to be able to reach out to these young people—as surely as He had given me breath, and I was certain that if I denied my calling, all of my other gifts would disappear. I know it sounds weird and syrupy, but I truly believed this.

I decided that I would continue on at Norfolk and fit the speaking engagements around my duties. I thought I could make both things happen, at least for the time being, and I jumped back into my old routine with an energy to match what I was bringing to my new one. I would not trade my duty for my passion.

I was so charged by this change in direction that my wife and I even attempted a reconciliation during this period. It was a fool move, born mostly of last-ditch frustration and can-do euphoria, but it yielded a wonderful fringe benefit—a beautiful baby girl named Maressa. The sadness was that the reconciliation did not last, and I was all the way out the door by the time Maressa arrived. I was back with her mother just enough to remind each of us that we could never build a life together, and I retreated to my couch determined to do something about it at long last.

Here again, though, I was rarely home long enough to make our divorce a pressing issue. I started traveling all over the map, all of the time. My wife and I were still not legally separated, but we were apart for all practical purposes. If I wasn't at the base, scrambling to get through my paperwork in double time, then I was out on the road, doing my thing in front of thousands of high school kids. When I was home during her pregnancy, I was either catching up on some seriously lost sleep or making up for lost time with Ashley.

At some point, it became almost a full-time job just finding a way to subsidize my appearances. I wasn't charging any money, and most of these schools didn't even have a budget to get me a plane ticket. Once I got to town, they'd put me up in a hotel or at one of the teachers' homes, but no one could really fund my travel. I was dipping into my own pocket more times than I could afford, but I never turned down a request because of expenses alone; some I could not do for scheduling reasons, but I would not let money become the issue. After a while, I figured that if I bunched a series of these presentations into one visit (at, say, three or four different high schools), then each school could kick in enough to fly me in. The only thing I insisted on was a high-tech sound system; without it, I would have blown out my voice on the first pass.

Each time I got back to Norfolk, I trotted out my

press clippings and letters and showed them to my C.O. He was impressed, but said he still needed me in my day job and that there were no funds available for my travel expenses. I even checked in with the people in the recruiting office and in public relations to see if there was some way we might take advantage of each other, but these jerks couldn't get rid of me fast enough. They'd pat me on the head (literally!), tell me what a great job I was doing, and show me the door.

The only things the brass cared about were making sure I didn't spill any classified information when I talked to the press, and making sure they didn't have to pay for any of this free publicity I was sending their way. Be a nice boy, they'd say. Stay out of trouble. Do whatever you have to do, but do it someplace else.

The problem was I was doing what I had to do in their own backyard. I was moving at full tilt, and there was no stopping me. I made a second trip to Baltimore (which this time included an appearance at my old high school), and I whacked that city so hard the military higher-ups couldn't help but notice. Most of the local television stations did a spot promoting my appearances on the six o'clock news. I made headlines in the papers: "Baltimore Boy Comes Back to Fight War on Drugs." Naturally, Baltimore is close enough to Washington that some Pentagon officials heard about my appearances and started to ask questions. What the hell's going on out there? they wondered. They didn't know diddly about a Navy-backed program for inner-city high school kids. They never heard of such a thing. Why weren't they notified? And where was the money coming from to pay for all of this?

My C.O. called me in for a dressing-down, but I reminded him that I was acting on his authority and that nothing had changed since we had first laid out our plan. "With all due respect, sir," I explained, "this is exactly what we talked about a couple months ago."

"Ah, but that's not true, Lieutenant," he said. "Now you're making waves. Now everything's changed."

Indeed it had, but there was nothing I could do about that. The whole speaking thing had kind of run away from me and taken on a life of its own, but I couldn't see pulling it back just to satisfy some unspoken rules and regulations. My boss was in a tough spot. He believed in what I was doing, even if he couldn't fully understand it. He didn't want to submarine my efforts just to save his hide—unless he had to. Finally, he asked me to go about things a little more quietly in the future, and I tacitly agreed. Of course, if an opportunity arose to call attention to what I was doing, I would have jumped all over it, but I didn't have to tell him that at this stage. I just needed to keep the Navy wolf at the door until I figured where this thing would lead.

By this point, Drew Brown and I had been making so much noise in our separate and joint appearances that the national media took notice. An NBC News producer was tipped to what was happening and sent a crew to Baltimore to tape one of our talks. He thought it'd make a good story—two black naval officers, strong-arming America's youth into staying off drugs and staying in school—and I tended to agree with him, so I made arrangements with one of the high schools for him to bring in his cameras.

Damn, I tore the roof off that high school auditorium that afternoon! I juiced everything up a notch for the network, knowing that if we didn't overwhelm these people with our presentations, they'd never do a piece on the evening news. I wanted the national exposure to force the military's hand. Once the word was out—on *NBC News*, no less!—I thought they'd at least have to kick in some monies to fund my travel. A part of me was even holding out for some high-level apology, for only indulging me in this pursuit instead of actively supporting me. Hell, in my dreams I even thought somebody'd create some special military post, allowing me to transfer out of Norfolk and tour the country full-time for Uncle Sam.

I raced back to Norfolk to brief the brass, but they gave me the same old runaround. This time I couldn't believe it. Here I was, making national news, and they still didn't want to hear about it! I went as high as the public affairs officer for the Atlantic Fleet, but all he seemed to care about was my assurance that I hadn't put my foot in the Navy's mouth and that I wasn't planning on doing so anytime soon.

It was not at all the reaction I was expecting. Come on! I thought. I'm set to be the subject of an extended profile on *NBC News* and invited to appear live on the *Today* show the following morning, in uniform! What more do they want? But all these guys could do was pat me on the head and hope I would go away. Soon.

Well, on Wednesday, June 15, 1988, when the piece aired on *NBC Nightly News* with Tom Brokaw, a curious thing happened. Apparently, someone had told the First Lady what Drew and I were up to and that our efforts would be highlighted on that evening's news-cast, and she made sure the President was watching the news. The Reagans were out in California that night, so they caught the news late, on the West Coast feed. The story that reached me the next day was that Mrs. Reagan was absolutely thrilled to learn there was a Navy program to support her "Just Say No!" campaign, and she passed her enthusiasm on to the President. Later that evening, President Reagan reportedly put in a call to Admiral Carlisle Trost, the chief of Naval Operations, and voiced his approval, and the CNO had to make like he knew all about it. None of his people had ever clued him in.

The very next morning, we were on the *Today Show* set, finishing up a live interview with Jane Pauley, when one of the production assistants came by to tell me I had a telephone call. A phone call? Here? My first thought was that something had happened to Ashley, or maybe there was a problem with the pregnancy. Why else would anybody track me down at a time like this? I had put in for the trip to New York; everyone knew what hotel I was staying at; people knew how to reach me before or after the show.

I took the phone and braced for the worst, but it was someone in the CNO office in Washington. I was so relieved that no one was hurt that it barely registered who was on the other end of the line. It was only after I'd hung up the phone that I realized how big this thing had become. This was the chief of Naval Operations! For a guy like me, it didn't get any bigger than this.

The CNO needed to see us that afternoon at the Pentagon. He said it was urgent. I hung up the phone and made to leave, but there was another call. This time it was from Donald Ian McDonald, the President's special assistant on education. He said "the White House" wanted to see us that afternoon.

Drew and I had already discussed going our separate ways and continuing with these talks on our own, but we figured we'd ride out this first wave of publicity together. After all, it was the two of us, together, that lent enough weight to our appearances to attract all this media attention. It made sense to milk it while we had the public eye.

We arrived in Washington just after noon and were escorted around the Pentagon like we'd just invented the wheel. I was glad-handed by one butthead after another—the same clowns who were patting me on the head and showing me the door just a couple weeks earlier. Before today, I couldn't even get them to write me a set of orders so that I wouldn't have to burn up my leave time to do these talks, and now they're jumping all over each other to claim credit for our "program." We weren't just two guys, on our own, crisscrossing the country talking to high school kids. No, now it was a "program," and everybody wanted in on it.

I never did get to see the President (something came up), but I don't think it would have mattered. I was so bitter about the two-faced reception of my superiors that I decided to resign my commission that same afternoon. Actually, to be precise, I made the decision that afternoon; I didn't get around to filing the formal paperwork until two weeks later, but in my head I was gone. These people wouldn't give me squat, and I wasn't about to let them in on the game at this point.

Plus, there was no way I could let their disinterest go unnoticed. One of my failings is that I can hold a grudge in a major way; if you burn me, I'll burn you back, and I'll make sure it takes you twice as long to heal. I'm not proud of this particular trait, but at least I recognize it and try to guard against it. This time, though, I didn't try too hard.

I knew I could find some way to turn these speaking engagements into a viable, self-sufficient operation. I didn't care about making money for myself, as long as I could provide for Ashley and the baby on the way. Already, I had dug myself a pretty deep financial hole. I had to sell a car to pay some expenses and go into debt to cover others. I used to give away some of my own money at these high school talks, to demonstrate that education and knowledge really *do* pay off, and these cash props really cost me, even in tens and twenties. I also ate some of my own travel costs, whenever I had to, and those plane tickets could pile up in a hurry, believe me. All told, I was probably running a $40,000 tab on my credit cards, which nearly matched my salary and benefits package.

Everyone in my life was telling me to stay put—my parents, my friends, my colleagues at the base. They all thought I was crazy to give up my commission for a half-baked idea that might or might not turn into anything.

But their objections were just another mountain, and I pushed them aside. I knew it would be tough, especially with all those bills to pay, but I also knew I could ride out the tough times if I kept the faith, if I kept on. One of the lines people fed me to talk me down from my decision was that my routine wouldn't work if I showed up at one of these high schools out of uniform—and once I was out of the Navy, I would always be out of uniform!—but I didn't agree. These kids didn't give a damn about the uniform. It was what I said that mattered, and how I said it. Sure, I was a little apprehensive the first time out in civilian clothes, but I simply stepped out in a jet-black outfit and jolted the room, same as always. I didn't need the stripes to help me do the job. I just did the job.

All I needed, starting out, was to build on this groundswell of interest and rethink some of the ways I managed my money. Oh, the interest was there, no question. Even before NBC, I had commitments stretching to the end of the year, and I knew I could fill in the blanks on my calendar once I let it be known that I was available. The folks at the network told me they took a couple thousand calls in the three days after my appearance, from schools looking to get in touch with me, so I was clearly in demand.

I was practical enough to put some of my plans on hold for a little while. There was no way I could meet all the medical expenses with the baby coming, so I arranged to stay on active duty through February 1989. The bills would have killed me if I was out on my own, and the Navy was happy to hold on to me in my new incarnation for as long as possible and by whatever means possible. Besides, I didn't mind taking advantage of them after they had taken advantage of me for so long. They moved me into a separate office, assigned me an assistant, and encouraged me to hit the road in what they were now thinking of as an innovative recruiting effort. All of a sudden, after all the press attention, the travel officers had found a way to pay at least some of my expenses.

Where was all this money when I needed it?

I didn't know whether to be thrilled or upset, so I decided to be upset. I guess I figured it would be much easier to have someone to blame if things didn't work out the way I was hoping—and not to have to share the rewards with an organization that had been way too slow to respond to what I was trying to do.

I don't believe that things happen by mistake. If you ask me, things happen because you make them happen. Things happen for a reason. God gave me the ability to stand on my feet and speak my piece, and it was up to me to put these tools to use. Whether by accident or design, I'd discovered that I could talk to kids in trouble and turn them around, and there was no denying it. Even if I could only make a difference for one student every time out, I had an obligation to that one student, and I could not turn my back on it.

And I believed I was destined to go it alone. What I really wanted was to find a way to build some type of speaking program into my job, to tour the country on behalf of the United States Navy. I didn't want to resign my commission. I wasn't out to make it rich or make a name for myself; I had everything I needed, and I knew who I was. But the Navy was my career. It was all I'd known since high school. I'd served my country for fourteen years—my entire adult life!—and the last thing I wanted was to shrink from such a powerful commitment or to break with such a huge chunk of my personal history.

But I didn't have any choice. After the lousy way I was treated, the uniform had come to stand for something different, and I couldn't wait to step out of it and into something new. I lit out on my second career with a heavy heart, but a clear conscience. I was giving up a lot, I knew, but I felt the Navy had already given up on me. I was just holding up my end of the bargain.

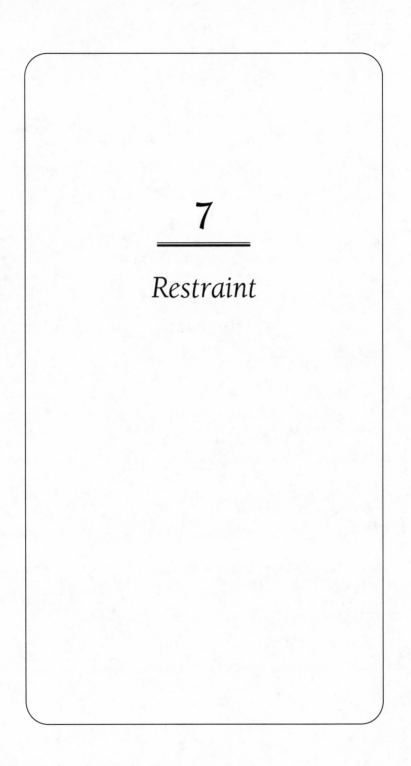

7

Restraint

Probably the best way to sell what I was doing in these presentations is to put you in the audience and let you hear me out.

I struck a number of key themes in my talks (family relationships, racism, drugs, teenage violence, education), but they all came down to the three watchwords that have guided my life since I was a small child: restraint, responsibility and respect.

I'll hit them one at a time in the pages ahead, and the first is as simple as it gets. Restraint. Look it up if you don't know what it means. For my purposes, it's stopping yourself from doing or saying something that might come back to hurt you or someone else. It's exercising control or moderation. It's pulling back when your impulse is to push forward. It's keeping you from making a fool of yourself—or at the very least knowing that what you're about to do is foolish as hell.

Here's what I think: if we teach our children simple restraint, we could solve half the problems facing young people today, easy. This may be an exaggeration, but I don't believe so. Kids today would rather lose their heads than use them. A whole lot of what's wrong in our schools—drug abuse, gang-banging, promiscuity, truancy—flows from an almost complete lack of foresight. I'm not advocating abstinence, not in the strictest sense, but I do believe we need to find the time to stop and think about what we're doing before we go out and do it. Obviously, kids are going to screw up whether they stop to think about it or not, but maybe they'll screw up less often, or maybe they'll learn something from it when they do, if they weigh their actions beforehand.

And it's not just kids who could use some restraint. We could all benefit from holding back, from reflecting on our actions before we commit to them, from saying no when we want to say yes. We can all do with some tempering every once in a while, whether in business or at home. Maybe there's something you're burning to say to your boss or your kids, but you know you've got to pick your spots if you want to be heard. Maybe you'd like to call in sick and head for the beach, but you know that if you do, you won't meet your deadlines or other obligations.

The choices we make are our own. If we all walked around doing what everyone else was doing simply because everyone else was doing it, the world would be a pretty sorry place. Kids face this dilemma most of all, through peer pressure and the pressures they place on themselves, but it doesn't have to be that way. I don't care what your situation is, there are things you can do to stay out of most kinds of trouble, most of the time. If you live in a bullet-ridden neighborhood, you don't have to hang out on your stoop every night with your friends. If your boyfriend wants to sleep with you, you don't have to give in when neither one of you has a condom and the drugstores are closed. If your mother works nights and your father's skipped town, you don't have to invite the crew over to your place to watch MTV. What you do have to do is be true to yourself, and pull back when something doesn't smell right. Think things through before moving forward. After all, the only time we can really undo our mistakes is before we make them.

I look back to my own high school experience, and I come up with all kinds of examples of times when I held back and times when I didn't. I wasn't perfect, as I've already chronicled, but I tried to strike a balance. When I messed up—and I messed up plenty—I usually knew what the repercussions of my actions would be. I knew the standard line about smoking dope, but I smoked it anyway. I knew it wasn't cool to run around knocking off convenience stores, but I looked the other way when my buddies were involved; sometimes I sat in the car and waited for them to get back with their six-packs, fully aware that if they were nabbed, I would be too. I knew that if I bullshitted my father, there was a good chance I'd get whupped. And yet I smoked dope, ran around and lied to my parents as much as the next kid.

Why? I've got no idea why, but I suppose in my stupid little head I figured the odds were in my favor. I thought I wouldn't get caught, or that marijuana would turn out to be not such a bad thing, or that the lies were worth telling to clear the way for good times I might not otherwise have had. Who knows what goes on inside a kid's head, but at least there was *something* going on in mine. That's the key, because when a kid just moves on his impulses without thinking them through, then we've all lost.

Sometimes I even thought things through all the way to a smart call, or turned a bad decision into a good one. I'll give an example. As president of my high school class, it fell to me to give a speech at our commencement ceremonies. Now, I happened to attend a high school that was as racist as any of the other schools in my area. Andover High School served a racist community, was run by a racist administration, and was attended by a racist student body. I believed this then and I believe it now. The few black students bused in from out of town were about as welcome in the halls of that school as an outbreak of lice.

The fact that I was one of the student leaders— active on the school newspaper, the radio station, team sports and school government—became a major source of controversy to some teachers and parents. But it was also a major source of my own self-respect. And it put me in a position to do something about whatever it was that was rubbing me the wrong way.

When the varsity football team wouldn't let a black kid start at quarterback, even though he was far and away the best at the position, I was able to quit the team in such a loud way that it called attention to the injustice. When a group of parents objected to the kinds of music I was playing when I spun records on the campus radio station, which was really just a co-opting of the school's public address system, I found a small transmitter and started broadcasting our signal off of school grounds as well.

Finally, a couple months before graduation, I set my thoughts down on paper and published a scathing attack in the school newspaper. It was, I thought, a perfectly justified criticism of a school district that was so completely out of touch with the times. Jesus, this was 1974 and parents still didn't want a black kid organizing the senior prom. The only part my sister could get in the school play was as the maid, when in truth she was probably the best actress up on that damn stage.

It was a backward place in desperate need of some forward thinking, and I decided I was just the person to dish it out. So I vented a little bit and let everyone know what I thought. My article was headlined, "The Air Is Filled with Racism," and it was the talk of the community when it came out. Unfortunately, most of the talk had to do with how the administration could have let such a diatribe find its way into print, and very little of it had to do with an honest reflection on what I was saying, but at least my friends were talking about it in ways that might have done some good. I didn't give a damn what the parents thought, or the teachers. I knew enough to realize that any real change would have to flow from the other students.

So it was in this context that I prepared my commencement speech, and my first impulse was to continue in the same vein. Graduation ceremonies were to be held in the gymnasium on the Baltimore campus of the University of Maryland, and the place would be filled with parents and community leaders. I thought it'd be the perfect place to deliver a classic parting shot.

People may have been able to tune me out by not reading the school newspaper or by refocusing their response so that it had to do with my right to publish my opinion rather than the truth of what I had to say, but this would be different. This time I would have a captive audience, and they would have to listen. It was, I thought, a perfect plan. I mean, how often did a black kid get a chance to run his mouth off to hundreds of white adults, each of whom was forced by propriety and circumstance to sit still and pay attention? Some of these people would even feel compelled to applaud, no matter what I said. How rich was that?

A couple weeks before the ceremony, I sat with our faculty adviser, going over my speech. This was part of the drill. I didn't have to clue this guy in to my agenda, but I figured I might as well. After all, I thought, where was the profit in getting up before all of these people and giving as good as I had if I couldn't also make them sweat a bit beforehand?

What I hadn't counted on was the adviser having anything worthwhile to contribute to the discussion.

But he was a good man, and as much as I hated it, I found myself listening to what he had to say. "Montel," he started in, after reading a draft of my speech, "this is a big day to a lot of people, a good day for a lot of people. It could be a good day for you too. I don't see why you have to go and louse it up."

He didn't tell me that I *couldn't* go out and speak my mind, but he did tell me that it wasn't such a good idea. I wanted to leave his office thinking this guy was just another in the long list of authority figures looking to beat me into the ground, but some of the things he said stayed with me. I went home and thought about them—really thought about them—and it started to seem that maybe slam-dunking all of these teachers and parents wasn't such a good idea after all.

Still, I went to graduation not knowing what I was going to do. I didn't talk about it with my parents or my friends, but I couldn't stop thinking about it. It was a big decision, and I could have gone either way. I had the vicious racist speech carefully folded in my pocket, and I had some innocuous little message committed to memory, and I sat through the opening part of the ceremony not knowing which one to deliver. I looked across the stage at my classmates, and I could see that some were crying. A lot of these kids were not going on to college; this was it for them, so it was a pretty special day. Then I looked out at the audience and saw a lot of the parents crying too. Some of them had been through hell with their kids and never thought they would reach this point together, so it was an important milestone for them too. Even some of the teachers were looking all misty-eyed.

All morning, friends were coming up to me, saying. "Don't be too rough, man," or, "Blast them," or whatever, all the time reinforcing that they were expecting me to come down hard. But as I was called to the podium I finally checked myself and realized that the real power in this moment would be in holding back. This was not the time or place to steam. I had done that in an appropriate forum, and it still hadn't gotten me anything. What was the point of kicking up that same dust here, now?

So I exercised a little restraint. The commencement people had set aside five minutes for my speech, but I only filled a minute or so. I said something gracious about my time at the school and the friends that I'd made, and challenged all of us seniors to go out and make something of ourselves, and that was it. Then I sat down to some polite applause and a palpable sigh of relief. I had the feeling that some people were still waiting for the other shoe to drop, that's how high expectations were running about what I would say.

I was clearly a better person for holding back that afternoon. I had no business muddying those waters on such a proud occasion. It was not the time or place, and it took me until the very last moment to recognize it, but I caught myself in time.

But do you know what? Even if I had gone ahead and pulled the prepared speech from my pocket and started ripping into all these people, it still would have showed a measure of restraint. I might have made the wrong decision, but at least I would have thought about it carefully before going ahead. At least I would have weighed the action against the reaction before setting things in motion.

That's how it is with restraint. Sometimes you stop yourself from making a fool move, and sometimes you don't, but you've got to pause to consider whatever it is you are about to do. Otherwise, we'd live in a world where consequences don't mean anything, when in truth the consequences are everything. If you're in the back seat of your car with your boyfriend or girlfriend, and everything's hot and heavy and clothes are flying every which way and it's clearly time to rock, there's got to be a tiny little voice in your head looking at the bigger picture. That's restraint. Sure, what you're doing feels great, but if you don't have protection, maybe you should just quit while you're ahead and save the rest for next time. Nothing feels so good that it should cost you the rest of your life.

And it's not just about sex. We all get our rocks off in different ways, and restraint comes into play in these as well. For me, when I was in the service, I used to get a tremendous rush in staying on top of my job and knowing more about a given aspect of our mission than anyone else. There were times there, when I was out at sea, when I thought I was the hottest thing going. I could do no wrong. It got to where my gut told me to make a decision without running all the information by my commanding officer. I was ready to put our ship in extremis just to satisfy my own ego. I knew that my instincts were on the money, but I also knew to feed the chain of command, so I pulled back and let the skipper make the call for me.

I didn't get the adrenaline rush of sticking my neck out, but I did the right thing. I took the prudent course. That's restraint. There were other times throughout my military career when my alligator mouth put my hummingbird ass in jeopardy, but for the most part I showed good judgment—and even when I failed to do so, I knew exactly what I was doing.

Sometimes in my presentations to high school kids, I let my confidence run away with me to where I lost control of the room or sent out some inappropriate signals. Why? Because I was too full of myself to let restraint stand on the same stage with me. The point here is that it's one thing to preach restraint and another to put it into practice. Oh, I've made some huge mistakes in my speaking career, and most of them had to do with my getting too caught up in the moment to accurately assess what I was doing; sometimes I didn't even try to figure myself out. For example, when Washington Mayor Marion Barry was first charged with possessing and using cocaine, I jumped a little too quickly to his defense in one of my talks. I was so hot about the way the media was cutting down our few black role models before they were even tried in the courts that I lit into Barry's accusers. It was only afterward, when I had a chance to sift through some of the angry responses of parents and teachers and consider some of the mounting evidence against the mayor, that I realized how irresponsible I'd been.

Restraint doesn't mean that you can't act with your heart, but you have to make sure your head's in the right place. You have to make sure you've considered the cause and effect of whatever it is you're about to do. And you have to pick your spots. There's a time and a place to speak out on any issue. There's a time and a place to do almost anything you want to do, as long as it's within the law. The trick comes in knowing when to pull back and when to go for it. That's restraint.

A lot of this goes hand in hand with responsibility, which I'll talk about next, but it stands on its own. Before you even have to take responsibility for your actions, you have to consider them. And that's restraint too.

So talk to yourself a little bit. Help yourself to think things through. Know that if you don't do your homework today, you'll be less prepared tomorrow. Understand what you're fixing to do before you do it, and grasp the consequences. And, once in a while, whether you're thinking of hooking school or lighting up or blowing off your curfew, tell yourself that maybe you don't need to do that today. Sure, it sounds like a kick, but you could have the same kick any old time. Maybe you should see what a kick it can also be to do the right thing every once in a while.

In the end, no one really knows what you put into a decision but you. You could follow your instincts your entire life and not get burned, or you could go with your gut and get nailed every time. But if you try to build your life around some measure of restraint in all things, then you're heading down the right road. From there, when something turns out right, you'll know why. When something turns out less than right, you'll learn from it.

These are the kinds of little victories that help define us as human beings. These are the things that are most important, because they help us to build to something bigger, something better.

8

Responsibility

Let me just continue with my riff on the three Rs, as I would on stage during one of my presentations...

The bottom line to almost every problem in our society today is that no one is willing to take responsibility for their actions or their future. The whole damn mess falls from this right here.

Think about it. We live in a world where there's an acceptable excuse for almost everything. Just flip around the news shows or scan the papers, and it will hit you full in the face. The evidence is best seen in the extreme. The Menendez brothers. Colin Ferguson. Susan Smith. Tonya Harding. Lorena and John Wayne Bobbitt. Hell, we won't even take responsibility for our elected officials; we voted them in, but it's not our fault if they don't do the job.

The big picture is maddening, but it is only a reflection of the smaller strokes. No one is accountable, and it's driving us all crazy. The bottom line is stooping lower and lower, and it has got to stop somewhere.

Perhaps the best place to turn things around is at home, in our own lives, with our own children. How do we do this? I don't have any easy answers, but I do have some clues. I do know that we carry the burden and the trust of our neighbor like a badge. I do know that all of us can, to a large extent, control what goes on in our own surroundings. And I do know that parents have a responsibility to teach their children how to exercise that control.

It is astonishing to me that in some cultures, throughout history, men and women have had to go before community leaders or tribal priests to receive permission to have children. I imagine that in some parts of the world this still holds true. What's astonishing is not that such a ritual was allowed to take hold, but that we've moved so far away from it. Here in the United States, in 1996, we have children becoming parents simply by virtue of their anatomy. Of course, this brings us to an entirely separate issue, but it reinforces how poorly qualified we are for one of the most important jobs there is.

What do we do about it? Well, responsible parents teach their children how to take care of themselves. They give them the tools they need to survive and thrive. They teach them how to hold a spoon, how to go to the bathroom, how to straighten their room.

Eventually, they teach them how to do their homework, how to treat other people, how to set goals and find ways to accomplish them.

I've tried to instill a sense of accomplishment in my own children from the very beginning, knowing that my own support and acknowledgment will only take them so far. I don't think it's enough to simply applaud your kids and root for them to do well. It's plenty, and it's a start, but you have to also teach them to root for themselves, to know that they can do whatever they want, and that true validation comes from within. A child's sense of responsibility flows from his own self-esteem, from knowing for himself that he can complete a task, or please his teachers, or motivate his friends. It's not the task itself that's important; it's the *knowing* that the task can be met and mastered; it's the confidence a child takes away from a job well done. These are the keys.

And while responsibility starts with the parent, it flowers with the child. Think back for a moment to when you were a kid learning to ride a bicycle. It's a universal memory that leaves even the most jaded human beings smiling, but in that memory is a rite of passage like no other. There's also a perfect object lesson. Try to remember what it was like when you were finally able to ride one hundred yards in one direction, one hundred yards in the other, and stop and start on your own. Chances are it felt great, but I'll bet there was more than simple pride at work. Part of the thrill probably came in knowing that for those few seconds, for one of the first times in your life, you were completely responsible for your past, for your future, for your health and safety and for the health and safety of others. No one could touch you but you. You were in complete control.

Granted, most five-year-olds don't recognize these feelings at the time, but I believe they're there, most definitely. They're undoubtedly the reason most of us look back so fondly on that moment.

Now, here's the point: if we all lived our lives trying to re-create that same sense of accomplishment, that same sense of responsibility, at least once each day, this would be a better planet and we'd all be richer people. Naturally, the stakes change as we move forward in life, but few things will ever be as difficult as that first trip around the block. Yeah, we'll fall once in a while, we'll scrape our knees, but we'll climb back on our bicycles and keep riding. And, eventually, we'll get somewhere.

It's all in the timing. To a kid, there's no bigger deal than learning to ride a two-wheeler, but it can only happen when you're ready for it. One week you're scared to death for your parents to let go of the seat, and the next week you don't notice when they do. The parent has to know when to let go, and the kid has to know when to take over.

In a way—to look again at the extremes— the same goes for the kid who's born, say, into an abusive family. In my own case, I wasn't big enough to stop my father from beating me. Another young lady might not be big enough to stop an uncle from sexually abusing her. But the moment will eventually come when the time is right to ask for help, when a child can step up and take responsibility, to try and turn things around. And in that instant, everything bad begins to get better.

It doesn't get good right away, and the bad may never go away completely, but it starts when we can stand up and say, "This doesn't have to happen to me anymore!" For me, it didn't happen until high school, but it happened.

Now, I hate to equate the joy of learning to ride a bicycle with some of the tragedies confronting families today, but I feel strongly that it is sometimes best to reduce even the most complex situations into simple terms. We are all born into different circumstances, and yet our concerns are mostly the same, at least at the core: we all want self-respect, self-reliance, self-indulgence. Maybe your mother's a crack addict, or your father can't hold a job. Or maybe it's not cool where you are to do well in school or to work for a better future. It all amounts to the same thing, and the remedy is no different from when you learned how to ride. You've got to pick yourself up, scrape yourself off and move forward. At a certain point, you have to realize that the only person responsible for your physical well-being, your mental health, your ability to get a job, is you. No one else gives a shit. I don't care if you have the most nurturing parents in the world or the greatest friends; it's still your face that stares back at you in the mirror every morning for the rest of your life, your butt that gets strung up when things don't fall the right way. You're the one who has to live with yourself.

So, what does this leave us? Maybe it's better to answer the question by looking at what responsibility *doesn't* leave us. For one thing, it doesn't leave us any convenient excuses. This is important. Sure, it's a lousy hand to grow up in a poor neighborhood, but it's not the worst thing in the world, and it doesn't have to mean the end of yours. There are better hands just waiting to be pulled.

How many poor kids don't take advantage of the one thing that's free in every community in this country—the library? How many kids don't assume responsibility for their own futures and go out and teach themselves one basic thing—to read?

It is anathema to me the way kids drop out of school like it's nothing at all. Black kids especially. What's up with that? Millions of people gave their lives to leave us the chance to go to school, to get an education. How dare any of us, with that kind of legacy, not be willing to learn how to read? To me, it's not even a choice; it's an obligation, and the duty rests with the individual. It's not the teacher's job to make you do your homework. It's up to the teacher to teach you how to do your homework, but it's your responsibility to take your butt to the library and not hang with your homeboys for those extra couple of hours. I don't care if you're black, white or green. It's up to you to do that little bit more, because if you don't, then your life will never be worth a damn.

Look, you could go out and win the lottery and become one of the richest people in the world, but you won't count if you don't take responsibility for yourself, if you don't set a path or a plan and dedicate your days to accomplishing something. It doesn't matter how much money you've got in the bank; it matters how it got there, and why, and what you plan to do with it. It doesn't matter what value society places on your life; it matters what *you* think. And it doesn't matter what you do or how well you do it; what matters is that you set out to be the best that you can be, at whatever it is you choose to do; what matters is that you try.

I'm tired of listening to young people whine about their lousy hands. People are trigger-happy to blame somebody else, or whole segments of society, for their particular dramas. Either you're contributing to the mass whimpering or you're as numb to it as I am.

"Oh, this happened to me because my father beat me." "This happened to me because we were poor." "This happened to me because I'm black."

Well, woe is me. Face up to it, people: if you're in the minority in this country, you will always feel like an outcast. Your children will always feel like outcasts. You'll have it tougher than most, most of the time. That's the way it's been, that's the way it is, that's the way it will be. Deal with it. I have long ago reconciled myself to the fact that some people will never accept me simply because of the color of my skin. And do you know what? I don't care. I truly don't. Accepted or not, I can still do whatever I want to do, whatever I'm qualified to do, whatever I'm entitled to do. I can supply my own validation, and I do that by setting a path for accomplishment and by assuming responsibility for staying on course.

No, nobody is going to give me anything, but I can earn any damn thing I want. If I want to be a lawyer, I can be a lawyer. You can be a lawyer too. All it takes is a high school diploma, a college degree and grades and test scores good enough to gain admission into a decent law school. And if I want to go to Harvard Law School, then I can do that too, but I can't bank on any kind of reverse discrimination or equal-opportunity quotas to take me there.

What's happening in this country is that we're no longer striving to perform at our maximum levels. We're mired in complacency, content to coast, to do what we need to get by and nothing more. And if we don't manage to get by, we'll find someone to blame for it. If we want to get into Harvard Law School, to continue the example, we'd rather find some loophole, as long as it has nothing to do with hard work and dedication. We won't take the responsibility to apply ourselves and meet Harvard's standards, but we'll look for the easy way in.

There's no denying that kids coming out of school today are facing a particularly tough job market, that for the first time in generations children will not have the opportunities their parents had. But I believe there's a reason for this. Colleges are turning out the first wave of students who grew up on television, who went home to empty kitchens because both parents were working, who had no one around to help them with their homework, who rode through high school on the backs of grade inflation and declining standards. We're in danger of becoming a mediocre society, shaped by mediocre minds, because we promote mediocrity in our schools. Each year, we graduate thousands of high school seniors with eighth- or ninth-grade educations, simply because school districts need to maintain their own pass-fail ratios in order to qualify for state or federal dollars. Even our most respected universities contribute to the problem, by depositing the tuition checks of subpar students.

When will it end? Most likely it won't, not on its own, not anytime soon. The problem will be with us until we all take responsibility for ourselves, for our children, for our communities. Children will never learn responsibility if they can't recognize it in their parents. If we take on the trials of our children as our own and hold them in trust until our kids can manage for themselves, then maybe we'll begin to turn things around. It's not a complicated formula. All you need is to make time in your busy schedules to talk to your kids, hang out with them, listen to them, understand them. If you don't have the time, find it somewhere. Get up an hour early, watch a little less television, make your child's interests your own. If at the end of the day all you can manage is an innocuous little question— "How was school today, Junior?"— then you can at least *listen* to your child's answer.

I am appalled at the way some parents have laid the responsibility for rearing their children on our institutions. I will never understand it. There are people out there who mortgage their futures just to conceive a baby. Or they run around in circles trying to adopt. They'd give everything they have just to hold a child and call it their own. But then there are parents blessed with as many children as they want, and they crank them out without thinking about it. Then they turn around and spend less than three minutes a day with their kids. They slop some food on their plates and send them off to school, hoping the teachers will know what to do with them.

Too many parents simply check out when a child reaches school age, delegating their responsibility to complete strangers. Luckily, most teachers and school administrators are caring and competent professionals, but there's only so much you can ask them to do. It gets to where when a kid is sent home with a black eye because he's been in a fight, the parent's impulse is to challenge the school, to rail at how such a thing could have been allowed to happen, when what really should be going on is a dialogue at home.

A kid left to flounder will grow up to be an adult without direction or hope. Let me offer a case in point. Recently, I decided to expand my horizons into the recording industry, looking to marry my lifelong love of music to my newfound clout in the entertainment community. If the paths I have chosen leave me in a position to do something else I've always wanted, then why not go for it, right?

Here's what happened. In my travels, I came across a singer with an incredible voice and enormous potential. This guy sounded like a collision of Michael Bolton and Michael McDonald, and he looked like Richard Gere with long hair, and when I met him, he was just bouncing around these small-town nightclubs and Holiday Inn lounges. He was itching for an opportunity, a chance to bust out, and I figured I'd give it to him. So we struck a deal: I signed on as the guy's manager, paid him a salary out of my own pocket, and started hooking him up with the hottest songwriters and producers I could find. Then I arranged for studio time and session musicians in New York and cut a demo to shop around to record labels.

Keep in mind, all during this time I was paying this guy $500 per week of my own money. (The idea was I would reimburse myself first, out of any monies we generated together.) His only job was to learn the songs, take care of himself, show up and give it his all. I paid for his trips to New York, for his studio time, you name it. I even arranged an elaborate photoshoot, with makeup artists and hairstylists and wardrobe people, to generate an appropriate portfolio to accompany the demo tape.

Finally, when we had two slammin' songs committed to tape, and the pictures were all printed up, I flew him back to New York to cut his teeth in front of my studio audience. He'd performed live before, but never in New York. We scheduled a dating show for the day of his visit, thinking we could set him up on stage to sing a love song in front of our panelists. (One of his demo songs had an appropriate lyric: "I'm waiting for my miracle to come.") We figured that if he could learn to play to a tough crowd—a talk show audience!— there'd be no stopping him. Plus, if all went well, we'd have a demo video I could send around with our demo tape.

I couldn't meet my singer's plane on the night he flew in, but he came to the studio early the next morning. My jaw dropped when I saw him. The man had grown a beard! It looked like shit, but that wasn't the point. The point was that I had just sent him to a talented hairstylist. I had just spent thousands of dollars on photos, trying to make a presentation to various record company executives, and he goes and changes his look on me. I still have no idea what he was thinking. (Probably he wasn't thinking at all, which was part of his problem!)

He knew we planned to tape his appearance on the show and to send out a video along with the demo. He knew it wouldn't cut it to have one look for the video and another for the pictures. He knew these record company guys would care about his appearance. They want to know how the talent is gonna look when they go to sell the album. They're not interested in some guy who doesn't know who he is from one day to the next.

And this wasn't the worst of it. When it came time for him to sing, he forgot the words to the song. I couldn't believe it. For three months, this guy's full-time job was to work on his appearance and presentation and learn two songs. That was it. I mean, how hard can it be to remember the words to two songs if that's all you have to do?

I checked out right there. I mean, I was gone. I'm not inclined to dish out second chances, not over something as basic as this. Either you want it or you don't, and it was plain to me that this guy didn't want it. I knew I'd never make him hungry to succeed. I couldn't stick success down his throat. I couldn't be bothered with holding his hand and calling him on the phone every day, making sure he's practiced, or worked out, or whatever. What did I need with that? Excuse me, this guy was the same age as me. If he couldn't take responsibility for himself or take charge of his own career, then it's not my problem. Let him cut his own deal. Let him be a lounge act for the rest of his life.

I'm sure this guy had a terrific excuse to explain away his screwups, but I don't listen to excuses. I can understand incompetence, I can understand stage fright and I can understand poor judgment, but I can't abide not trying. Good things come to those who try. Nothing comes to those who don't. I've had enough of all these people blaming each other for their difficulties; whatever their situation is, it's everybody's fault but their own. And when the blame runs along racial lines, it really rankles. If I had a dime for every black kid who stood up during one of my presentations and complained about how he could never amount to anything because his great-grandfather was a slave, or because he was raised in a cold-water tenement, then I'd have a lot of dimes. It's such nonsense! The real reason these kids will never amount to anything is that they've never picked up a book. So maybe it's not your fault that you were born into the ghetto, but the fact is, in most cases, it's your own lazy butt that's keeping you there.

What's most galling is when I interview a real gang-banger who's so far removed from taking responsibility for himself that he can't even see what he's got to work with. Seems to me you've got to be pretty smart to rise up and lead one of these inner-city gangs, to get other kids to carry out your orders. I spoke to one kid who claimed to be the most powerful gang leader in Chicago. His story checked out. He wasn't especially big or tough, but he had about thirty gang-bangers working for him, each of whom had another thirty or so people working under them. Now, that's a pretty sharp kid. He had bills to pay, loans to collect, deadlines to meet, territory to protect. He already knew the basic principles of any business in America: the spirit of entrepreneurship, the laws of supply and demand, the powers of persuasion.

This kid had it down, and if those brains had been applied to getting a good education and staying in school, there's no telling what he might have accomplished. And yet when I talked to him, he was filled with so much anger that he could never see the truth of his own situation. As smart as he was, he still said it was the white man's fault he was out on the streets. Man, this kid was full of this poisonous crap. I wanted to grab him by the collar and rattle some logic into him, but I knew it wouldn't do any good. A kid like that will leave this world the same way he came in. He might die with a couple thousand bucks in his pocket, cash, and some fancy jewelry around his neck, but he's not going anywhere, and the reason he's not going anywhere is that his parents never took responsibility for him and he's never taken responsibility for himself.

Now, I'm not blind to racism. It's out there—still, as much as ever—but it doesn't mean we can check out and quit trying. The truth of the matter is racism is no longer the obstacle it once was, and in my book it is certainly no longer an acceptable excuse for any of the failures plaguing some of our young people today. I'm sorry, I just don't buy the way kids are so quick to pin their troubles on their parents or on the color of their skin. Yes, I can see that you're black. I can see that you've got it tough, that no one's ever cut your father a break. I feel for you. I really do. But you can do better. In fact, it's your responsibility to do better. It's your job to take your rear end off the streets and sit it down in school or in a library, where it'll do you some good.

That's what it comes down to. There are no shortcuts in this world and no handouts. We've all got the same shot at the brass ring. Sure, some people have certain advantages, but so what? If you work hard, if you stay on course, if you take responsibility for yourself, you'll get to it eventually.

9

Respect

Stay with me one more time, and I'll touch all the bases in my standard routine.

A friend of mine once told me he posted signs around his house to remind himself and his family that it was okay to disagree with each other as long as they were considerate about it. It was a simple thing, but it was everything, and I adapted it to my own life immediately.

That friend was Caldwell Williams, a successful motivational speaker who put his ideas into practice. His motto was "Speak without offending, listen without defending," and he plastered it on his refrigerator, where no one could miss it. Then he asked his wife and children to pause at least once during any argument, as he would do himself, to visit the kitchen and ponder these words.

In my house we've hit on a simpler message: "R-E-S-P-E-C-T." I've spelled it out, just like Aretha, right there on the fridge. We can't miss it for trying. Respect. It is, truly, a word to live by, central to virtually every type of relationship: husband-wife, parent-child, brother-sister, employer-employee, friends, neighbors. Embrace it, and expect it in return, and you'll eliminate more trouble spots than you ever knew you had—at least those involving other people. (Back taxes, questionable taste in clothes, lack of direction...those I can't help you with here.) It doesn't matter who you are or what's at issue; if you respect the other person and take care not to say anything you might regret (or not wish to hear yourself), you'll see your way to a solution soon enough.

Set aside for the moment the notion of self-respect, or respect for certain institutions or other people. Right now, what I want to focus on is respect as a communications tool, because I've come to regard this as the foundation of everything else. One of the most glaring problems I've noticed, after talking to thousands of families across the country, is that people just don't know how to talk to each other anymore. I don't know when this happened—or how, or why—but there's no denying it, and it runs to our most basic disagreements. Let's say your child comes home from school on a Friday and asks if he can go to a party at a friend's house later that evening. If you're like most parents, your first instinct will be to say no, before you even hear your child out. That's disrespectful and adversarial. If someone treated you the same way, you'd be mad as hell.

Instead, in a conversational tone, tell your child about your concerns. Ask him what kind of party it's going to be. Will there be adults present? If so, which ones? What about older kids, from down at the local college? Which of his friends will be there? When you've gathered all the information you can, let your child in on your thinking. If you still want to say no to the party, that's fine, but you have an obligation to your child to explain your decision, and to explain it truthfully. If you're uncomfortable that there'll be no parents around to supervise, tell him why. If you don't like the idea of him hanging around with college kids, give a reason. It might set him off, but his end of the bargain is he has to show you the same respect you've shown him.

The key is including your child in the decision-making process. It's a reciprocal deal: he respects your authority, you respect his intelligence. At the very least, you'll get a dialogue going. You might find out what's really bothering your child is not this one party, but that he feels you don't trust him. He might find out that you do trust him—it's his friends you're not too sure about. So why not shoot for a compromise? Maybe you can have a party at your house. You can promise to stay upstairs, out of the way, and your child can promise to follow your rules. If the music gets too loud, you'll be down to tell him about it. If it gets too quiet, you'll be down to check on that too. This way, he gets to have his party, and you get to go to sleep knowing your child is safe, under your own roof.

Now, I understand that real life is not as simple as this, that the whole point of hanging with your friends on a Friday night is to get away from your parents, but I set this out only as an example of how we can respectfully navigate our way through almost any situation—an argument with your spouse, an impasse with your boss, a clash with your kids. At home, the burden is on the parents *and* the child. If you want to be treated like an adult, you've got to take some responsibility here. For some kids, in some circumstances, this isn't always easy, but it is often doable. Even if you live in the kind of house where your father gets angry just because you have the nerve to open your mouth, there's a way to approach him that won't put him on the defensive. Speak without offending: "Dad, when you have the time, I would really like to sit and talk to you about something."

It sounds simple (I know) and stupid (I know that too), but you'd be amazed at how little room for common sense there is in common practice. And you'd be amazed at how many parents would still be unavailable to their kids after a mature, reasoned approach like the one described above. Let me tell you something: if your kid asks you to make some time, you better make some time. And soon. If you don't, then damn it, that's the last time that child will ever look to you for anything. He's gone. Next thing you know, you'll be going down to the police station, or the abortion clinic, or the drug rehab center. Or the morgue.

Realize, I'm not by nature an alarmist, but the canyon that exists between most parents and their teenage children is alarming. And yet most crises can

144

still be avoided with a little respect. Sometimes that's all it takes. Parents, start in on your kids when they're young. You can't just tell a five-year-old to make his bed and expect it to get done. That's not fair to the kid. But if you tell your child why he needs to make his bed, and teach him how, and help him through it the first few times, you'll give him the tools he needs to meet the task.

Here again, include your child in your thinking. Help him to understand what the ramifications are going to be if he doesn't at least try to make a good job of it. Work with him to establish an appropriate punishment. If he suggests five minutes without television, tell him why that's not good enough. If he balks at your idea—say, five days without television—listen to his objections and be prepared to modify your position. Together, you can arrive on appropriate middle ground.

Curfew is always a big problem with teenagers, but it can frequently be solved with better communication. Okay, so your kid never makes his eleven o'clock curfew. Why? He'll tell you it's because there's nothing to do until ten o'clock at night. You ask him if there are things he might do a little earlier. He says, yeah, he could go to the movies, but the movies are expensive, and he doesn't have the money to go every week. Well, now you have a choice. You can either ignore your child's concerns or work with him so that he might answer yours. It cuts both ways, so why not float him a little extra money so he can go to the movies with his buds? Maybe you can give him a little job to do around the house, to make up the difference.

The point here is that you've got to find out what your child needs in order to accomplish your shared objectives. And you've got to get a dialogue going. Tell him why you want him home at eleven o'clock; listen to his arguments against; help him to understand your thinking and work to understand his. It's not enough just to tell him what you need. It's not even close.

We need systems of communication in every relationship if we hope to make them work, and the best one I know is to just post a simple reminder someplace where you can't miss it. R-E-S-P-E-C-T works for me, but you can come up with your own buzzwords to cut through the muddle. At home, tape them to the refrigerator or the bathroom mirror. At work, put them over the watercooler or program them onto your company's E-mail screen. Then, whenever there's a conflict, take a five-minute breather and go to the refrigerator or the watercooler and remind yourself there's a way around it.

I once spoke at a junior high school outside Philadelphia where the teenage pregnancy rate was off the charts. There were about seventeen or eighteen pregnancies in that one school, and I sat down with some of the administrators to see what was going on. Quite a few of these girls were victims of sexual abuses at home, and this was tragedy enough, but the real shocker was that in many of these cases the girls set out to become pregnant. It had become kind of a vogue thing in that community for a young girl to be pregnant. They'd look at their friend who was knocked up by her asshole uncle and see all the attention she was getting, and want some of it for themselves. They sure as hell weren't getting any attention at home or from the school, so why not try it this way?

Before long, some of the girls started targeting the most popular boys ("Oh, Frankie makes pretty babies," "DeShawn is cool") and comparing notes on their progress. They didn't have a relationship with Frankie or DeShawn or whoever, but they wanted their babies, and they were pretty calculating about it—poking holes in their boyfriends' condoms and lying about their periods.

This was what was going on, and it seemed to me the whole sorry business flowed from a monumental lack of communication. Nobody respected these girls enough to set them straight. Their parents screwed up, and their teachers screwed up, big-time, and it would have been so easy for things to fall another way. Of course, simply taping a phrase on your bathroom mirror will not eliminate the problem of teenage pregnancy in this country, but I strongly believe that in this junior high school the number of pregnancies would have been drastically reduced if adults took the time to talk to these kids in a way they could really understand. Oh, I'm sure there was some counseling going on and some efforts at home, but these were most likely argumentative and shot through with authority. No kid is going to listen to reason when an adult comes at her from on high, not over something like this.

What we have here, to pinch a line from *Cool Hand Luke*, is a failure to communicate, and kids are falling victim to it every day, in every community. I'll offer one of the more disturbing instances from my too-long list. I happened to be in Florida talking to a high school

147

group just a few weeks after a student had committed suicide there. The suicide was all these kids wanted to talk about, and after my presentation one of them came up to speak to me privately.

"I think probably he regrets it," he said, meaning the kid who killed himself.

"What?" It struck me as a pretty strange comment, and I did not know how to respond.

"Derrick, man," the kid went on, "I think probably he was just committing suicide, you know. I don't think he wanted to kill himself. I think it just got out of hand."

Now, hold on just a minute. How is it that a high school student cannot know the difference between the act of committing suicide and suicide itself? To this kid at least, the act and the end were two separate things. "I think he probably regrets it." What is that?

Stop and think about this a second. How many adults had to drop the ball for an impression like this to take hold? How little respect must parents, teachers, counselors and clergy show our young people for them to find a distinction between killing themselves and *trying* to kill themselves? (Maybe the kid was so confused he thought his friend was just *pretending* to kill himself.) I listened to this young man and could not believe it. Committing suicide, to him, was like an extracurricular activity. Hey, Chuckie, whattya want to do today? Man, I don't know, what say we commit suicide?

What the hell is going on here? I wondered. What the hell is missing?

Respect, that's what's missing. This kid was so clue-less he couldn't even buy a vowel, but he didn't get that way by himself. He got that way because he grew up in an environment in which nothing was kept from him, and nothing was explained. He got that way because his parents, his teachers, and even his friends didn't respect him enough to help him make sense of the world. They didn't respect him at all. They might have meant well, but a true line of communication cuts deeper than right and wrong, cause and effect, good and evil. I only spoke to this kid for a few minutes, and right away I could see he was in trouble. How a parent or guidance counselor could have missed these same signs is beyond me.

Think of the children in your life. How many of them are left alone in front of the television, assaulted by countless violent images and acts of degradation? It's easy to blame cable television or MTV, but it's every-where—prime-time network programming, the evening news, even some of the more lurid afternoon talk shows. Hell, when my older daughters are with me, I don't even let them watch my own talk show without me around to explain it to them.

When I was a kid, we watched *The FBI* and *The Mod Squad*, but that was about as graphic as things got. They showed guns going off, but they never showed the dead bodies. The network newscasts when I was growing up were fairly explicit—I'll never lose the images from the streets of Alabama and Georgia, of cops opening up those fire hoses on protesters—but I didn't know too many kids who were allowed to watch them in a vacuum. Political assassinations, the civil rights movement, the war in Vietnam...these things were discussed openly in every classroom, and most of my friends could discuss them with their parents as well. I know I could discuss them with mine, and I wasn't exactly raised in the most progressive home in Baltimore.

No, back then we couldn't see Rodney King being beaten to a pulp, on videotape, one hundred times a week, but we had our Rodney Kings. We had our race riots. We had our cities torched. Today, though, there's no escaping these scenes, and we've left our children to absorb them on their own. Kids don't even have to wait for television anymore. They can walk out on the streets of any city in America and soak up this stuff firsthand. It's all out there—drugs, poverty, crime, sex—and our children are right in the middle of it.

Another nightly news image that's been burned into me is one from the autumn of 1994: thousands of city kids, forced by their parents to pay their respects to a child laid out in a Chicago church, a victim of gang violence. What stays with me about that scene is not the nightmare of looking on the dead body of a small boy gone wrong, but the deeper tragedy of parents desperate to connect with their children, to keep them from the same fate. It was as if these people were not willing (or were unable) to talk to their children about what had happened, but expected them to be scared straight by the idea of it. They dragged their children down to that church to put a human face on a faceless struggle, but I can't imagine the experience resonated for any of these kids unless it was also accompanied by some serious, two-way conversation.

Communication, that's the key. And I'm not talking about lectures or diatribes. That's one-way communication, and it's destructive. It may have worked once, a generation ago, but it doesn't cut it anymore. Our children will not respond to dictatorial messages—we've told them by our own actions that they don't have to—but they will respond to authority. They will contribute responsibly to the decision-making process, if given the chance. They will listen to reason. If we treat our children with respect, and we treat each other with respect, then maybe something good will filter down.

The truly sad piece to this is that most kids don't know from respect unless it's presented in the negative. To disrespect someone, on the street, has become a cardinal sin, but the virtue is not given the inverse status. Why? Well, I don't know but I do have an idea. I believe it has to do with an overall decline in values. The moment we decided that lotteries and quick hits would be our fortune, the moment we set aside the notion of hard work for one of instant gratification, that's when respect checked out of this society. The two can't exist side by side. If you resent having to work for a living, then you can't possibly respect yourself, and if you can't respect yourself, you can just forget about the people around you.

We teach each other disrespect every day. Our President lies to us; our elected officials avoid us; our merchants ignore us; and our rich friends move into gated communities to keep us at bay. New York Yankee pitcher Jack McDowell gives his hometown fans the finger as he walks off field; Sinéad O'Connor tears up a picture of the Pope on national television; Olympic athletes club their opponents in the legs to improve their chances. We might as well pass another amendment to the Constitution and make it the law of the land: everybody has a right to disrespect whoever he wants, for any reason at all.

That's the way we're living. That's what we've become. I'm no one special, but I recognize these failings in myself and work to correct them. I have disagreements with my wife, and I say no to my children, but I keep coming back to that message on my refrigerator: R-E-S-P-E-C-T. I listen to them, and they listen to me. We solicit each other's opinions on important decisions. We give each other every consideration, and when we miss our marks, we just double back and try again. We keep at it. We try.

In the office, every day, I make an extra effort to treat people with respect, and I think I'm usually pretty successful at it. My problem is I expect the same in return, and when I don't get it, I'm gone. I don't care if people are rude to me or insensitive, but I can't stomach a lack of respect. Show it to me one time, and I'll have nothing to do with you from that moment on. I've severed lifelong friendships after just one infraction. Perhaps I should be more forgiving, but I'll work on that in the next lifetime. In this one, I'll just expect others to treat me as I treat them. If they can't manage that, they can't manage me.

Respect, by the book, suggests concern, thoughtfulness, the quality or state of being esteemed, or held in high regard. That's fine, but by me it also means trust, honesty, the ability to keep an open mind, to interact with others without rancor or disdain.

Without it, we're nowhere.

10

Talk Show

So there I was, crisscrossing the country for over two years, speaking to more teenagers than a census taker could count. My life was a blur. I couldn't tell one Ramada Inn from another, one high school from the next, one season from the one that came before. I was on the road more often than not, sometimes pulling into four or five towns in any one week. And in each town I'd cram as many appearances as possible—usually one in the morning, one in the afternoon and one (for the entire family) in the evening.

Let me tell you, my voice and my nerves were pretty much shot pretty early into this routine. But I kept at it because at that time, I truly felt this was what I was meant to be doing. I may have stumbled onto it, but there was no denying that I had a gift, a calling; if I did not answer it, I thought I would die. Just as a writer must write and a painter must paint, I had to be out there delivering these positive messages to high school students. It was who I was. I was blessed with the God-given ability to get kids to listen, to put them on the right track, to wake them up before it was too late. If they didn't hear the truth from me, they weren't going to hear it from anyone else. I had it in my head that I could change the world, one kid at a time.

I should mention here that it took a while for me to stop thinking of myself as a military man. In some ways, that persona came off with the uniform, but in others in lingered. Even today I sometimes define myself by my career in the military, and I suppose I always will. After all, that's what gave me the platform and the credibility to speak out on all of these issues. That's what I was about for longer than anything else. Still, I knew I would have to break from that place in my life if I was going to make this new effort work, and so I began to play down my military career in a lot of my talks. I stopped wearing my uniform. I didn't hide anything, and if the kids wanted to ask about my time in the service when I opened the floor to questions, then that was fine, but I wanted what I had to say to stand on its own.

What I had to say was basic: stay in school, stay off drugs, set realistic goals and work to accomplish them. I expanded on my themes of restraint, responsibility and respect to include the hot-button issues facing each community. If, for example, I was booked into a

high school in Medford, Oregon—one of the most seg-
regated stops on my tour—I challenged the kids in the
auditorium to dismiss what I was saying simply on the
basis of the color of my skin. This was the kind of town
where if you're black you wouldn't want to stop on the
one main road after dark, but I baited the audience into
accepting me and what I had to say. And they did.

If I happened through a town like Cincinnati during
a heated local debate on abortion, I forced the issue in
terms I knew would get a reaction. I said there were
probably a dozen kids in the auditorium who were living in such squalor and hopelessness and devastation
that they should have been aborted. And I meant it.
These were harsh words, I knew, but they made a compelling point: if we're looking to force our young people to have children, then we have to give them the
tools to care for them and to take care of themselves; if
we don't, we're miles down the wrong road.

And so it went, from one town to the next. I lived
like a nomad. I was never in any one place for more
than a couple nights straight. I set up a nonprofit organization in Denver, to be close to my new friend and
mentor, Les Franklin, and I had an office nearby, but I
had no real home. I managed to get back to Virginia
Beach every few weeks, to see Ashley and Maressa, but
in almost every other respect I had no personal life. I
spoke to my parents from time to time, and to my siblings on rare occasions, but I didn't run around, go to
parties, or hang with friends. Even the people who
knew me well had no idea what I was up to. I didn't do
anything but work and travel and decompress.

I was in a kind of holding pattern that stretched

on and on and on. While I was in the middle of it, I didn't think to mind, but it was a strange way to live for so long. It was like I'd stepped off the planet. So much of those two years are lost to me now, and all the things I did kind of run into each other in memory, but I don't regret a single second because that period was what brought me to where I am today. I just took things one yard at a time. That's the way I thought about it when I stopped to put it into perspective. Every day I moved another yard. Every day I made a little headway, I impacted in some positive way on some group of kids. Every day I inched a bit closer to…something.

To what, I could not be sure, but I figured I would find out eventually. Until then, I took my fuel from the small successes I made along the way. Oh, I got mail-bags of letters from all over the country: kids telling me I had helped to turn their lives around, parents thanking me for lending my voice to the positive chorus, teachers and administrators writing to let me know they were spreading the good word to their colleagues in the next town. Every week I'd hear from a dozen kids who'd enlisted in the military after listening to me talk, and while I did not want to be seen as being on some kind of recruiting kick, I still took this as a sign that I was getting through.

Probably the most compelling signs were the turned-around expressions on the faces of the most jaded students. These were what kept me going, more than anything else. Each time out, there'd be at least one kid who marched into the auditorium like the world owed him a damn apology. He'd sit way in the back, with a look that said, "Yeah, right, show me something," and I made sure I showed him something. I played to those kids and brought them around. I didn't need the letters from parents or the nods from administrators, but I needed to get these hardened kids to soften up to where they could face what was happening to them. If I didn't get through to each and every one of them, each and every time out, I would have quit, no doubt about it. The exhaustion would have gotten to me, the frustration. But that never happened.

Looking back on that period, I realize that I was probably running away from the situation at home as much as I was headed toward a new target. I was still sleeping on the couch on my trips back to Virginia Beach to see the girls, and no closer to a divorce than when I was stationed there. My Denver office was hardly furnished; there were no pictures on the walls. I either slept in a hotel or crashed with a friend. I had no idea where this itinerant lifestyle would take me, where it fit into my bigger picture, only that it did. I knew I couldn't go on like this forever, but at the same time I never thought to question it or to remove the uncertainty from my situation. I simply pressed on. Everything else would take care of itself.

After a while, I noticed a few things. Every time I breezed into town, there'd be television cameras all over the place. Some of these communities were so small that my appearance there was seen as big news. I don't mean to strut, but that's how it was. It wasn't too often that a former naval intelligence officer, someone who'd been written up in major newspapers and profiled on the network news, paid a visit to some of these out-of-the-way places. I made good copy, and I gave good sound bites, and each appearance generated a ton of publicity. The good word just spread and spread. Typically, there were three or four local news crews out at each high school, banking footage for the six o'clock news. Sometimes the field producers brought back so much tape that I could catch whole chunks of my presentation on the late newscast back in my hotel room.

This was both a good thing and a bad thing, although I didn't see any downside just yet. The upside was immediately apparent. When I was invited down to Jacksonville, Florida—in March 1989—one of the local television stations wanted to simulcast my appearance to the entire northern Florida area. I thought it was a great idea. In addition to the direct hit I'd make with students in the auditorium, I'd also reach a dozen other high schools in the area, live, on local television— maybe twenty thousand kids—in one afternoon. It wouldn't have the same impact, I knew, but at least it would get my message out there, and spare me some of the wear and tear on my body. And, for the kids who would only catch my act on their classroom monitors, it was better than nothing.

I decided to grow my presentation a little bit for the simulcast and incorporated a talk-back element to the program. I handpicked a panel of kids and parents and pulled them up on stage to debate some of the issues. It was, I thought, a logical extension of what I was doing. Already, I'd been having groups of kids come up and act out different scenarios, to illustrate whatever points I was trying to make, and the one just kind of led into the other.

Well, the Jacksonville presentation, broadcast on WTLV, was such a huge hit that I started getting calls from other television stations in other communities around the country. WTLV was a Gannett television station, owned by the same people who publish *USA Today*, and when we were honored with a "Best of Gannett" public service award, it seemed that every station in the chain wanted to borrow a page from our blueprint.

I wound up doing similar simulcasts (or guest-hosting on local public affairs programs) in Baltimore, Washington, D.C., and Detroit, to bigger and bigger audiences, and finally it hit me what was going on. These people were making money off my butt—big money!—and I was too stupid to realize it. (Hell, they were even selling commercial spots during my presentations!) This was the downside to all the television exposure, but I moved quickly to tilt it back up again. I didn't know squat about television, ratings, and advertiser dollars, but I was a quick study, and I determined to turn things to my advantage. I thought that if I could do these regional broadcasts once a week, or even once each month, then I could cover the country in a fraction of the time it would take on my own, the old-fashioned way. And I could sell or barter commercial time to underwrite my costs. Or, better yet, I could find a corporate sponsor to foot the whole bill and leave a little something extra in my pocket at the end of the day.

The money was important. I'd been collecting honorariums for each of my high school appearances—ranging from $500 to $5000—but the dollars didn't stretch very far. I had a full time staff of three to support, I had all kinds of travel expenses, and I had to pay for my own props and equipment. (I still gave away money in my presentations, and the tens and twenties added up pretty quick.) I also liked to kick back some of the proceeds to the sponsoring school—usually twenty percent of the honorarium—to establish some worthy program as a show of follow-up support or to fund one already in place. After all of this, I was left with a modest salary that barely matched my military pay, but now I had no medical benefits or job security. Economically, I was moving in the wrong direction, and once my wife and I at long last set our divorce in motion, I was looking at a mountain of legal bills and related expenses, and there was nothing in the bank to use as a cushion.

Understand, it was one thing to forsake a profit for the good of the cause, but quite another to go through the same motions and watch these television executives get rich as a result. I was busting my tail for the kids, not for the media honchos, so I took control of the situation. I did not swear off these television appearances entirely (that would have been foolish), but I stopped giving away my presentation. I started to think in terms of what television could do for me, rather than the other way around. I would appear on local public affairs shows, for a fee, to talk about dropping out or drugging out or whatever was relevant to the area. I would produce special interactive presentations, in roundtable or talk show format, at the station's expense. And I would do all of these things with an eye toward gaining maximum exposure in front of a camera, thinking that I might someday parlay these efforts into a gig of my own.

The mountains here were my own ignorance and inexperience, and these were easy enough to get past, once I recognized them. Like most people entering a new field, I was too trusting of those on the inside and not trusting enough of my own instincts. I knew what was best for me and these kids. I knew what I needed to get my message across. It didn't take a custom-designed suit and a master's degree in broadcasting to figure out how the television industry worked. All it took was the balls to ask questions and to stand up for what I believed, and I had those big-time.

A few of these local productions were particularly successful. One, at WUSA-TV in Washington, D.C., was featured on a regularly scheduled public affairs show called *In Our Lives*. They had me on to guest-host, and I brought on several local teenagers to talk through some of the problems they were facing at home, at school and on the street. Another, a special called *The Fourth R: Kids Rap About Racism*, produced for KCNC-TV in Denver, was nominated for a local Emmy, and when I won the award in September 1990, my world changed yet again.

By this time, I had already attracted a forward-thinking corporate sponsor, Pepsi, which had launched a two-year community affairs campaign around my appearances, so I was well positioned to shake things up. And now, with an Emmy in my pocket, I felt I had the validation to make a move. The award told me I could do whatever I wanted, so I started shopping similar program ideas to stations in Dallas, Chicago, Detroit…anywhere I could find a hearing.

My realistic hope was that I'd establish a local franchise in one of these markets and develop my own after-school talk show for kids. My unrealistic plan was to build a portfolio of enough of these one-shot shows to get myself a meeting at one of the networks or with one of the big syndication outfits. I was willing to start small, if that's what it took, but I didn't figure on staying small. I had quickly realized that the real reach in television was on the national level, but I was in no rush to get there. I simply saw these local gigs as stepping-stones to a bigger deal.

I slowed down on my speaking engagements and revved things up on the television front. I didn't want to abandon the high school talks entirely, but the constant traveling was sapping me of my energy and focus, and I knew I would have to cut back if I ever hoped to move ahead in other areas. I took it down to where I was on the road maybe once or twice a week, instead of every day, and at each stop I tried to build some broadcast component around my appearance.

About a month after winning the Regional Emmy, Pepsi asked me to tape a motivational prologue for a special scholastic version of the then-current Civil War epic *Glory*, to be shown to high school groups and youth organizations across the country. It was another powerful validation of what I was trying to do, and a unique opening to the television community. Freddie Fields, the Executive Producer of *Glory*—and a

Hollywood player—saw my introduction to his picture and asked to meet with me. He said he liked my presence and what I stood for. He liked the way I came across on camera. And he liked some of my ideas for an after-school talk show.

Freddie Fields introduced me around town—to studio and network executives and independent producers—and in less than three weeks managed to drum up serious interest in a talk show project. I don't know how he did it. Within three months, I had a deal with Viacom. We would go into preproduction in May 1991 and be on the air in June.

It all happened incredibly fast—so fast, in fact, that I was persuaded to lower my standards and shift my goals. I was blinded by the lure and promise of television, and a little less confident than I should have been. I'll backtrack and explain. All along, my idea for a youth-oriented talk show was being met with some resistance at the studios. Paramount, Viacom, Tribune …everyone seemed to like me and the way I came across, but they hated the concept. I wanted to call the show "Bridging the Gap, with Montel Williams," and they looked at me like I had two heads. They were polite enough about it, but they were clearly looking to move in a different direction. Then, as now, daytime television catered mainly to women aged eighteen to thirty four, and no one thought there'd be enough of a teenage audience to sustain what I wanted to do. And forget the audience: they thought I'd run out of kid-driven subjects a month or two into the show. "Montel," they'd say, patting me on the head with the same deprecating superiority I used to get from the military brass, "we know what works. This is our area. Why don't you leave it to us?"

So I did. To be fair about it, the Viacom people were always straight with me about what direction they wanted the show to take, and they made it clear to me what I was getting myself into, so I had no one to blame if things didn't work out according to my original plan. I just figured if I gave them what they wanted, I'd be able to get something back in return—you know, do a few shows for them, and one for me—and that's how it's been. They indulged me at first, encouraging me to produce one youth-oriented show every week or two, but when these proved popular, they encouraged me to do more, to where now they essentially leave us alone on creative matters. (Indeed, at this writing, the most successful afternoon talk shows are geared almost exclusively to teenagers.)

After nearly five years, we know what works and what doesn't, although at first I had no clue. We did two practice shows, before we launched the real thing, and it didn't even occur to me to ask what the little red light meant on the top of each camera. I just stupidly assumed the lights were on all the time, when in fact they were supposed to cue me to which camera I should be playing to.

Our first shows were a mess, but we got better at it each time out. I learned what I had to know on the fly. Every day I went down to the set and had the technical people walk me through the operation. I asked foolish questions. I offered foolish suggestions. I had to learn these people's jobs to where I'd be dangerous enough to know what I was talking about. (Television crews, I quickly learned, are suspicious of on-air "talent" who know what they're talking about.) It took a few weeks, but I got there. I learned about remotes and live feeds and satellites. I learned about cutaways and packaged pieces and audience research. For a former military cryptology expert, a lot of the technology was fairly standard stuff, once I made the leap in applications, and a lot of the programming considerations were basically common sense, but I even picked up on the subtleties before too long. I found out how much things cost, and why, and where we might save money for future shows. I learned what topics had been done to death and where to find a fresh approach. I figured which topics worked best for our show and which to leave to the rest of the pack.

We began a thirteen-week trial run on June 28, 1991, on stations in New York, Los Angeles and Seattle. We were just a small-time operation to start, but our presence in the top two television markets in the country left us smelling like a national talk show. (In syndication, a national program is one that is shown in at least 85 percent of U.S. television markets.) We were being written up in some of the major newsmagazines and featured on CNN, and people across the country had no idea who I was.

Naturally, without true national exposure we had a hard time booking guests, but we were also handicapped in this area by our Los Angeles base. To do an issue-oriented talk show from the West Coast is to operate with one hand tied behind your back. Man, it's tough. You're three hours behind everyone else, and it comes into play on almost every story. The news breaks on the East Coast; book tours start on the East Coast; the national agenda is often set on the East Coast. Either we'd have to get into the office at four o'clock in the morning or risk looking like a rehash of every other talk show on the air. I can't tell you how many times we'd send one of our producers out on a story only to find that the principals had already committed to another program.

Still, we managed to put on a show. And another. And another. By mid-July, we were broadcast in fourteen of the top twenty markets across the country. A second thirteen-week commitment took us through the end of the year, and during this time we added another dozen stations. We lived from one ratings book to the next, not sure if we would survive long enough to become a success.

A word or two on the talk show landscape at the time. Back then, there were only four established competitors for daytime audiences: Geraldo Rivera, Sally Jesse Raphael, Phil Donahue and Oprah Winfrey. (Actually, there were five, if you counted *Live with Regis and Kathy Lee*, which was subject to the same syndication ratings index.) But the airwaves got pretty crowded, pretty fast. After our brief summer tryout, we were joined on the air by Chuck Woolery, Ron Reagan, Jr., John Tesh, and a few other wanna-bes, but we continued to grow, even in such a pitched battle. We looked different than the other shows, because we kept coming back to stories about families and teenagers and relationships. Viewers who stayed with us came to know us as the last place to look for titillating or sensational subjects.

Let me tell you, the pressure to bend to ratings was enormous, and we occasionally fell back on the staples of the genre for a boost. One segment stands out. We had been on the air about four months, and we were beginning to pull decent numbers in our various time slots. This was almost a mixed blessing for a show like ours, just starting out. Once we demonstrated that we could draw an audience, we had to hold that audience and build on it. If we didn't, local station owners would slap a M*A*S*H rerun in our place so fast we wouldn't even see it coming.

And so we pandered. One of my producers pitched a show on infantilism, a typical tabloid topic that had rated well in a recent *Donahue* broadcast. She had a couple of guests lined up—adults who liked to dress up in diapers and suck on bottles—and a relevant mental health expert, and she walked me through what the segment might look like. As I listened to her pitch, I kept thinking that this was completely off the chart concerning the direction I wanted the show to take. This wasn't what we were about. If we couldn't be about kids and the complicated issues surrounding growing up in a complicated society, then at least we could explore adult subjects in a helpful way.

"No way," I said, after the producer presented her idea. "No way am I doing that show."

"But *Donahue* rated through the roof," she countered.

"I don't care about *Donahue*. I care about *The Montel Williams Show*."

"Well," she argued, "if you care about *The Montel Williams Show*, then you'll have to start doing shows like these sooner or later. You might as well get it over with."

I started to question my instincts. I was surrounded by all these people with afternoon talk show experience. I was only four months into their territory. I was pretty full of myself, but even I had to admit that some of these people might know at least a little bit more about this business than I did. I didn't think I'd be able to get through a show like this with a straight face—the plan was for several of the guests to come out on the set in their diapers—but I figured I could find a way to handle it if I had to, and almost everyone was telling me that I had to.

I did the show in protest, but I did the show. (And I put my foot down about the diapers!—our guests came on in their regular clothes.) It went against everything I believed about my new role, everything I was trying to accomplish, but I allowed myself to accept that a show like this could keep me on the air long enough for viewers to find out what I was really about. As it turned out, most of them already knew. The infantilism show turned in our lowest rating ever. (I believe it's still the lowest of the low.) People tuned it right out, and I liked to think it was because they had already come to expect something more from me. They could find grown men who like to dress in diapers elsewhere on the dial. From me, they wanted real people, talking about real issues, in real terms.

Like I said, I was a quick study. The day after that show aired, I sent word to my staff, to my producing partners and to my bosses at Viacom that I would have the final word on show topics. I would exercise my creative control. I slammed doors and yelled myself hoarse until I'd made my point, and from that day forward I've had a direct hand in every single one of our shows. If something didn't sit right, I moved on to the next thing.

Over time, our viewers began to see me as a straight talker. If a guest was in trouble, I'd try to get him some help. We gave our experts time to fully air their views in a substantive way. We refused to whip our studio audience into the kind of hootenanny frenzy that you sometimes see on other talk shows. We aimed to produce thoughtful, supportive, high-minded programs on topics central to every community: spousal abuse, teenage pregnancy, gang violence, infidelity, job retraining, fad dieting. From time to time, we'd throw a celebrity show into the mix (we did several, early on, with various soap operas, and one with the cast of the CBS sitcom *Evening Shade*), but we tended to set our sights somewhat higher than our competitors. It wasn't enough just to book an actor so he could plug a movie or television show. They had to have something to say, some way for my viewers to connect.

We didn't always hit our mark, but at least we had our eye on the target. And the viewers responded. The second thirteen-week commitment rolled into a third, and a fourth, and we were finally able to convince Viacom to move our operation to New York, and roll us out with a full-year commitment, as a nationally syndicated show, for our second season. I still had a lot to learn, but for the first time I felt we were making a difference and that we would be around for a while.

Now, finishing our fifth season, we're still here. The landscape has changed, and in some ways we've changed with it. Ricki Lake, Jenny Jones, Maury Povich, Jerry Springer and myself have kind of supplanted Phil Donahue, Geraldo Rivera and Sally Jesse Raphael in the ratings books. Oprah continues to beat all, but her numbers have slipped as she too resists the impulse to get down and dirty with the rest of the pack. Every year there are new pretenders to her throne. Marilu Henner, Richard Bey, Suzanne Somers, Charlie Perez, Rolanda Watts ...At one point in the 1994–1995 season, there were as many as sixteen nationally syndicated talk shows vying for the same time slots, viewers, guests and advertiser dollars. Let me tell you, it's a fairly intense competition. Most new shows don't make it past thirteen weeks, and the ones that stick have had to resort to sensational stunts and an ambush style of voyeurism that has lately fallen under attack.

But in the most important ways, I've resisted change. Oh, we've taken some heat for some of our more lurid topics, and some of that heat has been justified, but for the most part our shows have returned to the familiar themes I used to sound in high schools all across the country. Our most popular segments hit closest to home, and I have found that audiences appreciate that I'm willing to sacrifice a few ratings points to do something I know is responsible. And, for those times I know I have to tally some numbers in order to keep my time slots and stay on the air, I try to find an accountable edge. If, say, I've booked a show about sisters fighting over the same boyfriend, I'll try to examine it as a communication issue at home, to get past the easy headline and look at what's wrong in some of these sibling relationships.

Look, I'm as guilty as every one of my talk show colleagues. We've all done shows we regret. But I think the difference with me is I try to learn from them and to never revisit the same mistake. Afternoon talk is a difficult racket if you're trying to produce good shows and offer sound information. Every day I have to sit with my staff and keep them from doing what they've been taught to believe is a good job. The thing is, I don't care whether a show rates as much as I care whether it matters, and if that's a tough distinction to sell in my own office, I can just imagine how it plays with the television executives who are still trying to get rich off my ass.

But do you know what? I don't care. I truly don't. I make good money, yes, but I'm not in it for the money. I'm in it, still, to make a difference, to change the world, one viewer at a time. Every time out, I can step onto my bizarre pulpit and get a message to millions of people. If the message takes, and I can help people to turn their lives around, then I'm doing my job. If it doesn't, then at least I've tried. If I have to sell detergent and snack food and little pieces of myself to stay on the air, it's just part of the bargain.

I can live with that.

11

Romance

I don't mean to come down too hard on some of the more scandalous and salacious topics we occasionally examined on the air, because one of these shows actually turned my life around—and turned me on to a fourth R, without which all of my talk about restraint, responsibility and respect seemed suddenly incomplete.

Here's the situation: I had been divorced for several months and working my tail off, and not really thinking about becoming involved in another serious relationship when one of our producers suggested a segment on mother-daughter showgirls. Fair enough. It was exactly the sort of show that afternoon audiences

loved—titillating, provocative and broadly appealing—and exactly the sort of show I hated, but one I
was willing to do to pull some numbers. I knew the
game, and this was how it was played; if I wanted to
stay on the air, I had to do a show like this every once
in a while.

This time out, I didn't mind the bending, at least not
in the end. We were still in our first year on the air, still
scrambling to get noticed, still doing the program in
Los Angeles. One of our producers had booked a
mother and daughter that only loosely fit the segment's
premise; the mother had been a burlesque circuit
dancer/comedienne, who went by the stage name of
"Bambi Jones"; when the daughter started performing,
she adopted the name "Bambi Jr." The mother hadn't
danced in over fifteen years, and the daughter was
looking to move on to other things, but they were an
articulate, photogenic pair, and we thought they'd be a
good counter to the other guests on our panel.

Mother and daughter showed up for the taping at
the appointed time and I went backstage to say hello,
as I tried to do with all my guests before each show.
Well, let me tell you, Bambi Jr. made quite an impression. Her real name was Grace Moehrle, and she was a
strikingly beautiful blonde. I took one look at her,
decked out in a skintight outfit and dark glasses, and I
was pretty much floored. By this time, I had inter-
viewed dozens of gorgeous women on the show—
models, actresses, dancers—but no one had ever
struck me in quite the same way. Grace and I chatted
for a bit, and underneath the small talk I felt an imme-

diate connection. I couldn't say for sure whether she felt the same thing, but I was definitely gone.

Now, I had never dated any of the guests on the show, and up until this time it had never been an issue, but I found myself thinking this was one of those rules that were made to be broken. (And right away!) For the time being, though, I had a show to do, so I tried to set aside my personal interests. This was tough, and fate didn't exactly make my job any easier. Midway through the taping, we were hit with a mysterious, full-scale power outage, and our lighting technicians scrambled to relight the stage. It was a mad, frantic scene, and for a while we weren't sure if we could salvage the day's taping.

Nothing like this had ever happened before (and it's never happened since), and at first there was no explaining it, but I just took it as a sign. The way I saw it, the lights went out so I could have a chance to talk to Grace, so I filled the downtime at her side, hoping to find that this sudden attraction was mutual. I ignored the rest of the guests, the studio audience, and the producers barking last-minute changes to our game plan, and focused my complete attention on this dazzling young woman. Man, I was rude and unprofessional, but I didn't care. I didn't even notice anyone else in the room.

Next thing I knew, about a half hour later, the lights were back up and we were ready to roll, but I was too far gone to do my job well. I stammered through the last few segments, all the time thinking I had to find a way to keep this woman in my life, beyond the taping. She had me thinking it wouldn't be easy. Already, during our brief conversation, Grace had turned me down when I asked her to dinner, but it wasn't a flat rejection. It was more of a "not at this time in my life" sort of rejection, so I wasn't about to give up just yet. She said she was involved with someone else, but indicated that the relationship was on its last legs. Plus, her body language wasn't what I'd expect from someone who was completely disinterested. She even planted a nice, wet kiss on the top of my head, later on in the taping with the camera rolling. There was something there, most definitely.

Now it was just up to me to find it, and catch it, before it got away.

So this was what was running all through my head, all through the taping. For all I knew, I was the only one imagining any kind of future between us, but I let my imagination go crazy. I didn't want to come on too strong, too soon, so I couldn't really ask Grace for her number. Besides, I knew I could always track her down through our production office, if in a couple weeks I decided to press my luck again. The key, I thought, was to just play it cool and see if anything might develop on its own.

And yet I wasn't so cool that I could let the moment pass. For some reason, I decided that if this woman drove off our lot before I could talk to her again, I'd have let a rare chance at happiness slip away. I set it up in my head that Grace—a woman I hardly knew—was my true and everlasting love. I could not let her disappear out of my life and back into her own, but I thought I'd have to kind of nonchalant my way into another encounter.

Quickly, I hit on a lame strategy. I had just gotten a sleek-looking Acura NSX (the car wasn't but a few weeks old), and I was still at the stage where I was taking extra special care of my new toy, but all that pampering fell away with Grace on my mind. I couldn't think of anything but talking to her some more, and when I saw her stepping into the limousine we had arranged to take our guests from the studio back to their hotel, I freaked. I couldn't think straight. I jumped into my gleaming new car, thinking I would pull around to casually wave goodbye, just as she was pulling away, except the way the parking lot was configured I had to jump a half dozen cement bumpers to reach her in time.

Understand, these weren't simple speed bumps blocking my path, but the hard-angled cement dividers that separate one parking space from another, the kinds with the names of studio honchos stenciled on the side. (Talk about overcoming serious obstacles at the start of a relationship!)

What the hell, right? I didn't give these cement dividers a thought. I backed my Acura across the parking lot to Grace's limo and pulled up alongside as slick as could be. I beat the sleek right out of my car—the chassis was all dented, the muffler twisted out of shape, the fender bent big-time—but all I cared about was making a good impression. Like a fool, I thought this would do it.

Somehow it did. I must have looked so pathetic that Grace took pity on me. That, or maybe the sparks flying from the collision of metal and cement somehow cast me in a not-too-ridiculous light. She still didn't want to have dinner with me, but this time her "no" seemed to be more about scheduling and less about something else. Actually, it was more of a "we'll see" than a straight "no" and I took this as another sign. There was hope for me yet.

Over the next couple months, Grace and I spoke on the phone from time to time—usually on my impulse, and my dime, but eventually on hers as well. She came into the office once, to pick up a tape of her appearance, and we sat down and talked for a bit, face-to-face. I was growing on her, I could tell. (Or, at least, her resistance was fading.) She still wouldn't go out with me, but we were becoming friends. We talked about our goals, and our dreams, and how we might help each other with each. We reached out on the very surface levels—I put her in touch with some Hollywood types who might help in her acting career; Grace introduced me to the actor Edward James Olmos, who wound up appearing on a show we did about gang violence in East Los Angeles—but we were also pulling for each other below the surface.

Finally, she agreed to go out with me. It wasn't the most romantic first date in the world (she insisted on lunch), but it was something. Strike that: it was everything. One lunch led to another, and soon enough to dinner, and suddenly there was no denying where we were headed. We talked all around it—what it would mean to our friendship, once our relationship took a sexual turn; how committed we were to the idea of each other; how what we both wanted, more than anything, was to settle down into a loving family.

Naturally, we talked about the difference in the colors of our skin, and it was an old conversation with a new complexion. We had both been involved in interracial relationships, but never in one that was so future-minded, so early on. It was clear to both of us that our getting together wasn't just a hot romance—although it was also that!—but a long-term commitment. There was an unspoken promise of something more, something lasting. We had to consider what our mixed marriage might look like, and the kinds of motions our children would be put through as a result. We may have been getting ahead of ourselves just a little, but to do anything less, we both thought, was to sell out our future for the sake of our present. We owed it to each other, and to the family we might someday build, to think of everything.

We went out and took an AIDS test together, and when the results came back negative, we waited and tested ourselves again. I think we both sensed that when we finally did jump into bed together, we wouldn't be jumping back out anytime soon, and we wanted to make sure everything was right. We'd waited this long to get together, so what was another few weeks?

This beautiful, romantic dance went on from about January 1992 through March, and all during this time we were cementing our friendship. Everything fell from that tight bond. We took two trips to Hawaii. We shared a room, but we didn't sleep together. We stayed up all night talking and cuddling. This was completely new ground for a hyperactive military man like myself, but I didn't think to question it. Hell, looking back, I would not have played it any other way. To be honest, I probably encouraged our holding back far more than Grace did, because I didn't want anything to spoil our time together. I wanted it to be perfect.

I wanted it to last.

And it has. (And it will.) We were married on June 6, 1992, in a simple ceremony at the Tropicana Hotel in Las Vegas. For a while, we talked about an elaborate wedding at the Naval Academy chapel in Annapolis, but the plans started to get away from us. It was becoming a big social thing, and a big business obligation thing, when the focus should have really been on the two of us, alone together. We weren't getting married for the rest of the world; we were doing it for each other, and if this sounds like a cliché, well then I'm sorry, but it truly felt like the more meaningful we tried to make the celebration, the more meaningless it all became.

And so, on our whim, we gathered the people who mattered most: my parents, Grace's mother and stepfather, my brother and his fiancé (my sisters couldn't make it on such short notice). My abiding regret was that my daughters weren't there, but they were too young to fly alone, and the logistics of collecting them and flying back out to Vegas were unworkable on our timetable.

As it was, Gracie and I barely had enough time to get there ourselves. We flew in on a Saturday morning, got married that afternoon, and flew back out the next day.

I was back at work Monday morning, so we didn't even have time for a honeymoon. We were in the middle of moving the show from Los Angeles to New York and taping my first prime-time special, so there was virtually no time to step off the wheel and savor the moment.

We stole what time we could. Grace came with me to the studio every day (she did my makeup) and started sitting in on production meetings and helping out wherever she felt she had something to offer. I was traveling a lot in those days, as we introduced the show into new markets, and she made every trip with me. We gave ourselves a crash course in each other—twenty-four hours a day, seven days a week. Right away, Grace became my most trusted adviser, because she was the only one around me who had my interests fully at heart. And her instincts were so solid I found myself wondering how I'd gotten along without her.

It was funny to me, and telling, the way the entertainment press reported our marriage. At first, I was astonished that my private life was subject to such public scrutiny, but this was the least of my concerns. All of a sudden, I was getting heat for marrying outside my race, as if I had to answer to some higher code, now that I was in the public eye. I couldn't understand it and tried to fit it into the bigger picture. I started paying attention to attacks on other well-known African-American men who were being beaten up in the press for their involvement with Caucasian women. Why was it, I wondered, that every time a well-known black man became involved in an interracial relationship, reporters were on his case? They seemed to think that a "successful" black man had an unspoken obligation to his African-American brothers and sisters to "keep up appearances." I had no idea how to respond to such nonsense, so I chose to ignore the questions when they were put to me. I mean, who the hell were these people—strangers!—to challenge me and the life I was living?

Besides, their theories about successful blacks didn't hold up in my case. I was successful long before I had a television talk show. I was successful before I became an officer in the United States Navy. I was successful back in high school. I dated white girls as a teenager, and nobody seemed to notice. My first wife was white, and nobody seemed to notice. Goodness, my mother was half white, and my daughters were of mixed blood, so I was pretty much color-blind in this area.

Of course, it didn't take much to figure why our mixed marriage was news, when the facts of my private life hadn't been news all along. The difference now was that my success had become public and trumpeted, and this was all the difference in the world. Now I was making it, on national television, in the mainstream of a stubbornly racist society, and I guess it was just too much for these (mostly) black reporters to see a black man in a solid, loving relationship with a white woman—plucked, presumably, from the same mainstream. It was like I was rubbing their noses in something, whereas before I was just going about my business, pursuing my own happiness.

The troubling part to all this was that there was a definite double standard for men and women. How many Whoopi Goldbergs or Diana Rosses will it take to balance out the mixed relationships of prominent black males? I'll tell you, there will never be enough. Black men will always take a bigger hit on this ground than black women. Why? I'm not sure, but I suspect it has to do with a basic fear that cuts through our society like a virus: white American males will not be outpaced by black American males on their own turf, and they will not see their women cross racial lines.

With Gracie and me, we confronted these issues head-on, early on. We felt we had no choice. We lived not only in the here and now but also in the days ahead. We had to keep our eyes focused on the children we would someday have, the community we would someday inhabit, the future we would someday hold. We had to think if people would accept us, if they would accept our children, if their children would accept our children. We had some very tough, very realistic concerns. Face it, this is America, and we would have been foolish to think we could blanket ourselves in love and gushy sentiment and pretend that racism didn't exist. But racism does exist, and I'm afraid it always will. It's a part of our world, and we had a responsibility to each other—and to our unborn children—to anticipate it and to find a way to deal with it.

Our children were here soon enough. Gracie became pregnant by the end of our first year together, and she gave birth to a beautiful baby boy on September 17, 1993. We named him Montel II, and for the first time in my life I felt a sense of immortality. It had to do, I think, with the complicated mess of male emotions surrounding the birth of a first son, but it also had to do with the profound attachment I had built with his mother. I looked at my wife, my partner, nursing our brand-new baby boy and thought, Through this child, our love will last forever.

I felt the link even more strongly the second time around, after the birth of our baby daughter, Wynter-Grace, on January 21, 1995. She is my little Grace, the love of my life in miniature, and magnified (if such a thing is possible!). As I write this now, I marvel at the ways each new day checks out richer than the day before, and it's because I go home each night—spent and exhilarated—to a house filled with love and laughter and respect. It's one giant miracle. I've never known anything like it and can't imagine anything to match it.

Oh, I love my two older daughters with all my heart, but I never had the chance to love them through their mother as well. Here, now, with my two younger children, I am doubly blessed, because in their eyes, and in their hearts, I find their mother, the love of my life.

All of which brings me in a roundabout way, to the central theme of this chapter: romance. Let me tell you, everlasting love takes work—even if it isn't exactly hard labor. After all the mistakes I'd made in my past, and after looking at dysfunctional families and couples all across this country, I've worked to make our relationship a model of how to love and care for another human being, how to communicate, and how to keep an open mind. Grace has worked at it too, and that I think is the essence. We are best friends, lovers, confidants. We are both committed to a lifetime together. I look at Gracie not only as the person who validated my worth but also as the person who has vested me with the power to do the same for her. It's an enormous responsibility, but unbelievably nourishing when it cuts both ways.

We'd both been involved in unhappy relationships before we got together, so the first thing we did was sit down and talk through every conceivable place our time together might take us. It was a simple thing, but it became the foundation of everything else. We talked about what was important to us. We talked about sexuality. We talked about our pasts. We talked about faith. We talked about communication. We talked about family. Nothing was out of bounds.

We entered this relationship talking to each other as friends about the mistakes we'd both made in our lives. We continued the discussion even after we were married and set down on paper what we called our post-nuptial agreement. To this day, Grace carries her copy in her wallet, as I do mine. We made a little joke out of it, but underneath the fooling there is an absolute truth. It is our contract to each other, our pledge of allegiance. We covered a whole list of things—most of them serious, but some of them less so. We promised to make time for each other. We promised not to get mad when we have to discuss something. We promised to give the other person the benefit of the doubt.

And we promised to always call each other silly little affectionate names—no matter how old and sorry-looking we eventually became. Right now, we call each other "Doo." This is probably the most embarrassing thing I've ever revealed, but I figure this book is all about being open and honest, so I might as well tell all. "Doo" comes from a Beatles song we both like—"Love Me Do"—and for some reason we bent the lyric a bit so that the "Do" of the title became our pet names. "Love, love you, Doo." Sometimes we'll be sitting together late at night, after the kids have gone to sleep, and Grace'll start singing it, and then I'll kick in and finish it. We'll just be sitting there singing, calling each other "Doo." (Like I said, this is pretty embarrassing.)

Now, I don't mean to suggest that we've covered everything in our soul-searching talks or in our post-marital contract, or that Grace and I don't occasionally hit a bad patch, because we're only human. Shit happens. Sometimes things get so crazed at the show that I lose sight of what's going on at home. Sometimes, if Grace has had a lousy day, she's ready to bust by the time I come in the door. But we try real hard not to take our frustrations out on the other guy. We try to draw strength from each other, instead of just laying things off on someone else.

If you're in a relationship and you want to make it work, you have to be a little selfless at times. I was selfish in my first marriage, most definitely, and this was one mistake I was determined not to repeat. Grace and I even got to where we set aside one or two nights each week to vent about work, or the kids, or whatever pressures are bearing down on us at that moment, and confined our complaining to those nights alone. This way, we can both have something nice to look forward to, when we're in the middle of one of our rotten days—and know that we'll still have time to vent a couple days down the road, when we're a little less caught up in whatever it is that has prompted us to vent in the first place.

One of the things that keep our marriage strong is

the element of surprise. I'm always trying to catch Grace off guard, to do the unexpected. Once, on Valentine's Day, I rented space on the electronic Sony sign in the middle of Times Square and plastered a personal message on the big screen. I made sure Grace was outside, looking in the right direction at the right time, and she was absolutely floored. Whatever your budget, and wherever you live, there are things you can do to get the same message across. Take out a personal ad. Get your lawn mower and cut a heart shape into your overgrown front yard. Cover yourself in Saran Wrap and put a bow on your head. Do whatever it takes to keep each other laughing and feeling appreciated. It's not enough, going back to this Valentine's Day example, just to send flowers or a card. Put some thought into it, some feeling.

Another thing I did, after our daughter was born, was steal Grace away for a weekend in a fancy New York hotel. She'd been pregnant for eighteen out of twenty five months, and I knew how hard it was on her, physically and emotionally. Plus, I wanted to let her know in a tangible way how much it meant to me—to us!—that she had gifted our family with these two wonderful children. So I ditched the kids with their grandmother, booked the finest suite, filled the room with flowers and ordered up a catered dinner.

And I didn't stop there. Grace was particularly sensitive about what the pregnancies had done to her appearance. I thought she looked beautiful, but she felt like someone else had rented her body for the last two years and now she wanted it back, so I asked the owner of one of her favorite boutiques to send a selection of outfits up to our room. The idea was that Grace would spread out all these clothes and start to feel good about herself again. I wasn't pressuring her to get back into shape, but I knew that was what she wanted, so I just gave her a little boost.

Now, I realize that not everyone has the means to do what we do. (Hell, it only *seems* that everyone has an afternoon talk show on the air or in development!) But you can take the same impulse and adapt it to your budget. If your wife does all the cooking in your home, sit her down on the couch one night while you fix dinner. Drive her to work one morning, if it means she can sleep in an extra half hour and not take the train. What counts is that we make an effort, that we step outside ourselves and put someone's needs ahead of our own. In cliché there is truth: it *is* the thought that counts, so think about it, by all means.

I truly believe that what goes wrong in most relationships can be traced in some way to neglect. Or forgetfulness. There are no mountains here but the ones we create for ourselves. We neglect each other's needs in favor of our own, and eventually we forget what it was that brought us together in the first place. Think about this, too. When we're falling in love, we're swept up in an enchanted, do-no-wrong kind of feeling, but then we get beyond all the lust and infatuation and lose sight of what bonded us together. We become selfish. We talk about what we want out of the relationship, and not about what we want to put into it. We forget what it was like the first day we met, when there were butterflies in the stomach. We forget what it was like the first time we kissed.

With Grace, I pray I never lose those butterflies, or that first kiss, but I know that prayer is not enough. I know that we can't just let our marriage alone and hope that it takes care of itself, because it won't. We have to tend it and nurture it, and work like hell at it. Every day we remember the reasons we fell in love with each other. Every day we try to trace those first butterflies. Every day we kiss each other, as if for the first time.

This, more than anything else, is what keeps us together, and strong.

12

A Message to My Son

15

A Message to My Son

Little man, nothing is easy.

By the time you are old enough to read these words, you will know this for yourself. You will know that the world your mother and I have brought you into is not the nicest place. You will know, probably firsthand, that there are people out there who want to cut you down because of the color of your skin, cut you off because they don't want to hear what you have to say, and cut you out because they've got some set notions about where you belong.

That's how it is, how it's been and how it will be, and it's up to me to help you find a way to deal with it. I've talked a lot about responsibility, and this right here is the biggest one of all.

Right now, you are so wide open, so ready to accept. You receive everything on its face, greet everyone with a smile and meet every challenge unafraid. You are a constant wonder to me, a joy to behold. Really, I watch you go about your days and thrill at the unvarnished way you interact with people. But I can see into the future. I am afraid that what Albert Einstein said is true: the tragedy of man is what dies inside a person as he lives. You are not yet two years old, and I am afraid that your pure, trusting nature will die, a little bit every day, from here on in. I am afraid that one morning you will wake up not knowing who to trust or what to believe. You will be tempted to see yourself as the rest of the world sees you. You will have to deal with the prejudices and hatreds of some very nasty people, and whether you buy into their stereotypes or not, you will still be tainted by them, in one way or another.

This tears me up inside. Why? Well, for a whole mess of reasons. Naturally, you're my son, and I want you to have every chance at happiness. I want things to go well for you—not easy, necessarily, but well. Your struggles are mine, exponentially, and it falls to me to smooth your way. Still, it's more than this, I know. Probably it has to do with the fact that you are the last Williams. My father was an only son, and you are his only grandson. You carry my name, and all our hopes, and with that I feel a special obligation to prepare you for what lies ahead. I will do the same for all my children, but for some reason ...I don't know, it feels *different* with you. I've never thought of myself as a male chauvinist, but I suppose in this way I am. Right or wrong, I've invested your future with more meaning than I have your sisters'. I'm not sure why. I love you all dearly, and equally, but there's something about a bond between a father and son that transcends all other relationships. I am your legacy. You are my future. We can be everything to each other or nothing at all.

I know that with my own father—your grandfather—it took me years to reach a place where we could be ourselves around each other. These days—at last!—we have a great, loving relationship. We talk all the time. We cry on the phone together and tell each other our secret triumphs and fears. We support each other always. My father and I had a hard time when I was growing up, as you will know, but when I hit twenty-five (the same age he was when I was born), I finally saw things from his perspective. He did the best that he could with the tools that he had.

It was tough for your grandfather—a black man trying to make his way in a white man's world—and he sometimes took out his frustrations on his family at the end of the day. Should he have found another way to deal with his anger? Absolutely, but you have to remember, this was back in the 1960s, long before we were all so attuned to our relationships and our feelings. This was the way my father was raised. This was what he knew. And, as a kid, it was all I knew too.

Now, as an adult, I can forgive my father for the way he sometimes treated us. Actually, it goes beyond forgiving. I understand the way things were for him. I feel what he felt. I know what he feels now. He may not have been the kind of man to take me in his arms and tell me he loved me, but there was love in our house. There was kindness.

What I'd hate more than anything is for you to have to reach twenty-five before we can find the same place in our relationship. I want to start now. Time is too precious. You are too precious. And we have too much work to do.

So, where do we start? How do you help a child grow up free of hate and at the same time arm him with the confidence and dignity to defy those same hatreds in others? How do you teach a boy to become a man? to filter the conflicting messages he gets on the street? in school? on television? Are you supposed to be hard or soft? tough or permissive? thick-skinned or sensitive?

The key, I think, is that there is no single right way to go. The only way to go is your own, and I'll be here to help you figure it out. Oh, I'm gonna fix your knee when you scrape it and hug you when you hurt, but that's just the beginning. I'll probably yell at you more times than we'd both like, and louder than we'd both like, but I'll make sure the right messages get through. I've built my life on discipline. Without it, we'll never amount to anything. With me, under my roof, it's gonna be a difficult road. I'll be as hard on you as I am on myself. I only hope that if I'm sometimes too rough, there'll be enough of a foundation between us that you'll understand. You'll know that I'm not riding you for any one reason, for any particular screwup, but for your future. I want to make sure that you have a future.

There are so many traps along the way, for a young black man, that with my own son I must be super-vigilant, at least until I know the right messages have taken. I listen to the statistics and I cringe: one in four African-American men are in some form of police cus-tody—jail, bail or parole. One in four! And that's not the worst of it. The worst is how the three-quarters of us who stay out of trouble are made to live with the taint of the others. Crime in America has a black face on it, and it will continue to have a black face on it for the foreseeable future. For all I've accomplished, and everything I've tried to be, a white woman will still cross the street late at night when she sees me coming. I'm still called "nigger"—in New York, in Los Angeles, in Beaumont, Texas. I'll never get what I deserve in this world, even as I get what's coming to me. You'll know the difference soon enough.

And you'll have it even tougher. You're a black man born to a black man in the public eye. You share my name and all the baggage that goes with it. There are people who don't like me just because I'm successful, just because I'm black, just because I have the nerve to breathe the same air as they do...and they won't like you too, for the same non-reasons. This is what you'll have to face, straight on and hard, but you won't have to face it alone.

And there's more. You're not only black; you're black *and* white. You share a wonderful bond with your mother, and you share her blood and her history. I pray this doesn't leave you confused, but enriched. I pray that you will know, within yourself, that you have the blood to make whatever decisions you want, to be whoever you want, to do anything. It can go either way, I know—either you'll fit in everywhere or nowhere—but I pray that you will remain open to the world and let the world see you as you choose to be seen.

Race is a big thing, but it's not the only thing. It's trying enough just to be a man. Kids today don't grasp how to set goals, how to figure their own course, how to do the right thing, because they're being pulled in so many different directions. It's tragic the way so many young men shrug off their responsibilities—as sons, boyfriends, students, fathers. They're being told to get in touch with their feminine sides, but they still don't treat their girlfriends with respect. They don't respect themselves, either, and that's a big part of the problem.

These things I can pass to you by example, by the way I live. I will give you the tools that I wish I had growing up, the tools your grandfather wished he had to give. I will teach you the three Rs. I will teach you discipline. I will teach you love and tolerance and faith. I will teach you to forgive. Some of these things I do not yet know for myself, but I will learn them, for you. I will be here for you, in every way I can. This is my obligation and my promise.

There's a song I hear on the radio every now and then—Harry Chapin's "Cat's in the Cradle"—and it blows me away every time. Lately, it just runs through my head on its own, without any help from the radio. It's all about a father who works his tail off, trying to provide for his family, and he wakes up one day to find his kids are grown and out of the house, into busy lives of their own. I don't want us to be like the father and son in that song, but I can understand the father's dilemma. Sometimes I stumble home late at night, thrashed from an out-of-town trip, and pull you into bed with me, to sleep on my stomach. Sometimes I'll wake you up early, to throw the ball around or play with your bubbles, if I know that's the only time we'll have to be together that day.

I work so hard right now—seven days a week; ten, twelve, fourteen hours a day—that I sometimes lose sight of what I'm working for: the freedom to be around for you in ways my father could not be around for me. Since the moment you opened your eyes in the delivery room, I have felt a profound sense of responsibility and purpose. It was something other than what I felt with your older sisters. Maybe the difference here is that you were my first child born into a loving relationship, or maybe you've unleashed some primal, male-bonding force in me. Whatever it is, there is no denying it. Before you were born, I was driven to work hard—to accomplish everything I could accomplish, to love my children—but the more your eyes glowed, the more I had to prove. It's a weird equation, and I haven't quite got it figured, but I am determined to provide for you and to be here for you, at all costs. I'm not there yet, but I'm trusting that I'll know when to give up one for the sake of the other. Give me some time.

I love you, Montel. I truly do. It may be that we get so caught up in the discipline and routine that we both lose sight of this beautiful truth, but I hope not, and if we do, at least you'll have it here, for the record. Your father loves you more than life itself. I would stop a bullet for you, or a train. I'd do the same for your sisters and your mother, but I want you to understand from me, man-to-man, that I would give up my life for you.

That you carry my name is a blessing, but I worry it might also be a curse. Your mother and I thought a long time about this, but in the end we decided that I am who I am, and you will be who you will be. My failures will not be yours, just as my successes will not be yours. I can't turn over any family business to you or groom you to replace me on the air. Even if I could, I wouldn't, because I don't think a man can respect himself until he makes his own way. You've got to build your own future, for yourself. You've got to keep your eyes open and focused—not on what your father's done, but on what you can do.

I hope to guide you, teach you, mentor you, shape you ... but I'm no role model. Your role model should be your own two eyes, staring back in the mirror. That is the shining example of who you should be and what you can become. Always be aware of everything around you. Be ever vigilant in everything you do. Look ahead. Look around. Know where you're going all the time. Know that there are people out there who look at you funny. Know why they look at you funny. Know how it makes you feel. Know that you deserve respect. Demand it, and if you don't get it, move on. If someone doesn't respect you, you don't have to deal with that person.

Above all, know that you have the hope of God in you, that you were placed on this planet to be the best that you can be. Look at yourself in the mirror and like what you see. Be proud. Know who you are. And know that I'll be looking back at you, always.

Remember: I am your legacy; you are my future. Together we can move mountains.